BUSINESS PLANNING
FOR NHS
MANAGEMENT

CAROLYN SEMPLE PIGGOT

The Health Care Management Series

Series Editor: Keith Holdaway

Performance Management and Appraisal in Health Services, Martin Edis
Managing Change in the NHS, Trudy Upton and Bernard Brooks
Business Planning for NHS Management, Carolyn Semple Piggot

First published in 1996

Kogan Page Limited
120 Pentonville Road
London N1 9JN

British Library Cataloguing in Publication Data

A CIP record for this book is available from the British Library.

ISBN 0 7494 2057 X

Typeset by JS Typesetting, Wellingborough, Northants
Printed and bound in Great Britain by Clays Ltd, St Ives plc

Contents

Contents

Preface

It is true to say that the term 'business planning' would not have been at home in the pre-1990s NHS, and even now critics complain of market-based terms creeping into Health Service thinking.

My own view is that this is wrongheaded. Of course the NHS should be based on the sound principles of equity and effectiveness and it should put the needs of patients and the public first. But more and more people are becoming aware that this can best be facilitated by adopting the proven methods of the business world.

Good business planning is the key to obtaining the clarity required to commission and to deliver what patients need and what the Health Services priorities require. Right across the NHS – from the NHS Executive to individual GP practices and clinical directorates – the analysis and monitoring required by business planning is taking hold and bearing fruit.

This book, written by a senior manager at one of the world's most successful companies, Glaxo Wellcome, offers an easy and well-defined route to effective business planning. I am sure it will be of great benefit to managers throughout the NHS.

Jean Trainor
Deputy Director, NAHAT

Acknowledgements

A large number of people have helped in bringing this book to you. I owe a great deal to the help, support and encouragement of my family, friends and colleagues: in particular Dr Amanda Pullen and Ann Jolly from their time at Glaxo and since; Jean Trainor at NAHAT; and above all, my parents for their lifelong support. This book would not have been possible without the participation, over several years, of NHS managers and clinicians in many organizations across the UK. Thank you all for making this possible.

NAHAT

NAHAT (National Association of Health Authorities and Trusts) is the leading organization working for NHS management bodies. It brings together NHS authorities, health boards and NHS trusts into one representative organization covering the separate and collective views of both purchasers and providers. It represents members' interests to Ministers and to other decision-makers. It promotes the benefits of the NHS and provides its members with a wide range of support services, research, conferences and publications as an aid to the delivery of high-quality healthcare.

Series Editor's Foreword

'Fitter, leaner organizations' has been the catch-phrase for the process of removing layers of middle managers from NHS organizations. For senior managers this has meant either taking on more work and facing personal burnout or delegating tasks and authority to staff who have not worked as managers in the past and who do not usually feel trained to do so.

The Health Care Management series is aimed at just such people: operational staff such as heads of department or localities in purchasing or provider organizations, ward sisters/charge nurses and their deputies who find that they are increasingly expected to deal with management issues which, until only recently, they were expected to refer upwards.

To complicate matters further, such delayering of our organizations has come at a time of the most radical alterations to the systems for planning, commissioning and delivering healthcare since the service was founded. The National Health Service seems rapidly to be turning into the 'National Health Business' with an ethos and methods that feel alien to many of the staff expected to live with them. The boundaries between health and social services become ever more blurred as care is increasingly delivered in or near to clients' own homes, upsetting established patterns of working just as new and inexperienced managers take over the reins. The new organizations that have formed are undergoing a period of rapid learning and team building to undertake their new roles.

Established service planning techniques, which always used to reside at District or Regional level, have been replaced by Trust level business for providers and by Health Authority plans for purchasers. As a result a great many more staff than before are involved in the planning process. This book explains the usual content and structure of business plans and how they can be used to safeguard healthcare outcomes as well as allocating and helping to control resources. By understanding how business plans are developed and used in organizations, members of staff can have greater control over their working life and environment by influencing the planning at an early stage rather than accepting the plan as a *fait accompli*.

Subsequent titles will reflect the general issues affecting all managerial or supervisory staff, as well as throwing light on the changes to healthcare in the UK to which they must respond. The authors have been chosen for their practical experience of dealing with these issues themselves, or of helping others to do so. The books in this series are therefore not academic treatises but working handbooks full of advice and practical aids. We hope that they will prove to be useful tools in the rapid personal development that will be needed.

Keith Holdaway
Assistant Director Human Resources
Mayday Healthcare NHS Trust, Surrey
1996

Chapter 1

What is Planning?

'Business planning is a management tool used in a systematic way for approaching future problems and overcoming them; it represents a qualified and quantified compromise between what a business wants and what it can actually achieve over a defined period.' (Deffenbaugh, 1990)

This chapter sets the tone for the book. Here I look at what planning is, both in a general context and for planning within the NHS. Planning principles will be illustrated by real-life examples, taken from around the country. By tackling planning in this way, I hope to show how the healthcare professional can contribute to the planning process – not only in the phase of creating the plan, but also to manage the process of buy-in throughout the organization and beyond; and, most importantly, in the implementation and measurement of the plan's success.

Some questions tax the minds of people in the commercial and public service worlds. These questions are common, but can be answered in different ways – not because of the difference between the organizations, but more to do with the people who work for or benefit from them.

The first big planning question is 'What makes a successful organization?' Success can be defined from the perspective of the people who work within the organization, the people who rely on the organization to provide them with some product or service (for example, healthcare services) or people who have a stake in the organization, other than employees (suppliers, share-holders, etc). What each of these people think success is can be very important in determining the way in which the organization operates.

A second key question for organizations is 'Why do some organizations stagnate and fail?' A successful organization is one that has vision. Later we will explore what a vision is, how to create one and how to ensure everyone working in the organization is committed to it. The alternative is an organization that stagnates and fails – often one where the managers and staff (and particularly the top team) are not committed to the vision or the plan.

The plan can often be considered by an organization to be its 'route map'. How else can it 'see' its destination, find the way there, and, more importantly, know when it has arrived? In order to plan effectively for its future, there are a number of questions that an organization must ask itself. These questions also guide each individual's contribution to the plan.

1. Where are we now?
2. Where do we want to be?
3. How can we get there?
4. How far have we got?

It is easy for us, as managers, to become so engrossed in current problems and day-to-day issues, or 'fire-fighting', that we spend too little time on longer-term planning. Our immediate need seems to be 'How can I deal with this crisis?', which takes up all our time and gives us little scope for considering the broader view. Further, we often fail to ensure the necessary involvement in any planning, whether short or long term, of any line personnel. Why are we then surprised that they are not engaged in the planning process or what the plan is trying to achieve? So our first lesson is to involve people from throughout the organization in the planning process – that way, we stand a greater chance of succeeding in what we are trying to do.

Short Term Versus Long Term

A short-term plan is one that can be described as an action or operational plan. It will answer the four planning questions we have just asked for the short term and be largely concerned with what is going on inside the organization. Strategic plans have a wider scope and attempt to answer these questions for the long term, and cover not only what is going on inside the organization, but also the external environment. So planning overall concerns both operational and strategic elements.

The most useful time-frame for planning is the one to three year time-scale. In a rapidly changing environment, such as the current NHS, it is difficult to forecast what is likely to happen in year five; plans designed for that type of time-scale are unlikely to be effective.

Corporate Strategy

Most commercial organizations, if not all, have some sort of corporate strategy. It has been described as 'the direction and scope of an organization over the long term; ideally, which matches its resources to its changing environment and, in particular, its markets, customers or clients, so as to meet stakeholder expectations' (Johnson and Scholes, 1993). So, it defines where the organization is going and 'cuts its cloth' according to prevailing market conditions. Some of the language is recognizably that of a commercial organization, but the principles can be applied equally well in the NHS context or, indeed, in other public services.

'Strategy is the direction and scope of an organization over the long term; ideally, which matches its resources to its changing environment and, in particular, *the internal market, consumers of services* and stakeholder expectations' (my emphasis) (Bower, 1995). Looked at another way, the following is applicable to both the public and private sector: 'The goal is not to create value for customers, but to mobilize customers to create their own value from the company's various offerings' (Norman and Ramirez, 1993). It is not what an organization thinks will work well for customers or consumers of its services, but what those customers or consumers make for themselves from what the organization offers to them. While that is the essence of marketing, it requires a good solid business plan for an organization to be confident that it has got it right!

3

The trademarks of effective planning are creative thinking, use of a planning process, sound knowledge of the organization and its environment, the choice and selection of different options and coordination of resources (people, time, money) to make it work.

In order to plan ahead, an organization needs to do two things; first, the production of a plan, including what is necessary, what is possible, how it can be achieved and what the organization would like to see as the results of the plan; second, what is done with the plan once it's written, the management required to see it through, the controls, processes, organization and monitoring required in order to give the plan the best chance of success. In this book we will look at each of these areas in turn.

Here is my first 'government health warning' – having a plan is not, by itself, a guarantee of success. To keep planning in perspective, it is helpful to remember that:

- Planning will not give you a 'perfect crystal ball', nor will it enable you to predict the future with extreme accuracy.
- Planning will, or should, minimize the degree to which you are taken by surprise and help you revise both programmes and activities whenever it is desirable to do so. In other words, planning will help you react both creatively and constructively to change.
- Planning will result in bringing together all the organization's activities and its best efforts towards reaching its objectives.
- Planning does not stifle creativity. Planning enhances creativity by providing an orderly process, which means that, providing the objectives and plans are realistic, there is a good chance they can be reached.

Six Planning Myths

Turning to what planning is not – rather than what it is – there are six common myths that should be debunked. How many times have you heard these when you've started your planning process?

1. 'There's one right way.' There isn't. There are a multitude of techniques and approaches, and different approaches will be right for different organizations at different times. Criteria for what constitutes a successful plan should be established before the plan is written.

   For example, if you were planning in the home entertainment market in Victorian times, your plan would include pianos, playing cards, etc and your success would be judged by how many households had these things. In the 1990s, you'd need to think of different things – a video, TV, hi-fi or computer would be more typical of the times.

2. 'Let's wait and get it refined.' You can always spend a lot of time in analysis, and discussion can continue ad infinitum, but a point is reached, and must be recognized, where further work produces diminishing returns. Two techniques that can help here are either to say 'is this 80 per cent right?' for example in terms of analysing the external environment (see Chapter 2); or to agree a date by which the plan has to be submitted, in which case the definite deadline focuses the minds of the planners.

3. 'We won't tell the downside.' This is the good news only story. Managers want to be seen in the best light and their planning may stress opportunities and strengths rather than threats and weaknesses. At the end of the day, however, they will be measured against the plan, so a realistic case should be presented. However, those who are working with the implementation of the plan need to be alert for changing assumptions. For example, in 1943, the then chief executive of IBM predicted that the total world market for computers would only ever be for five machines!

4. 'The income will come, or the costs will be controlled.' This was a prevalent point of view during the 1980s. It is easy to assume that revenue will continue to rise or that costs will continue to fall. However, circumstances change, and any assumptions, such as market conditions continuing as at present, should be explicitly stated so that deviations from the plan can be accounted for.

5. 'Let's not get too committed.' This is a particular problem now more than ever. With the idea of 'portfolio lives' and changes to work patterns many people now believe they will only be in a job for a few years before moving on and therefore feel

they do not have to be fully committed to a long-term plan for which, by the end of its term, they will no longer be responsible. In practice, 'You're only as good as your last... ' applies well here, unless you wish to establish a reputation for poor planning, and decrease your chances of employment in future.
6. 'Planning is a one off!' So many plans end up dusty and unread on shelves and seem to bear no relation to the 'real' day-to-day work. The completion of a plan should really be viewed as only the beginning. A successful plan needs to be continually monitored and reassessed against the constantly changing environment. In reality, changes to the plan are often only written down once a year with the new planning cycle.

By avoiding these pitfalls in thinking the planning process will happen and should be successful.

Why Plan?

At this point it is probably helpful to look at the rationale for planning, both in a 'commercial' sense and in a 'public service' context.

> 'At an early stage, authorities need to establish a vision of where they are going and an explicit statement of the values or philosophy that guides their work. In addition, they should develop operational strategies for achieving long-term objectives. Another key function is to agree procedures for monitoring progress towards objectives and for keeping track of performance.' (Ham, 1991)

Planning is needed because the environment in which business is conducted is becoming increasingly complex. Changes to the environment, whether they are technological, political or market driven, are becoming more frequent. One of your roles therefore, as managers and healthcare professionals, and one that is increasingly important, is to look at, and assess the impact of, the changing environment, and to provide a framework for decision making in which the organization can adapt to its new environment.

Whether you are a purchaser, commissioner or provider in the new NHS, planning for the future is a major requirement to ensure that resources are deployed efficiently and effectively, providing appropriate healthcare on an equitable basis, ensuring access for all who need it and meeting social acceptability.

Why Do We Need a Healthcare Plan?

While there is general recognition that planning is a good thing for commercial organizations there are some who remain sceptical about the value of a 'business plan' for public services. To convince those people, there are a number of reasons you can give. First, a plan is essential to communicate to all stakeholders (see Chapter 7 for more information on managing stakeholders) and to get collective agreement to the set direction for the organization. Second, it provides a basis for obtaining and allocating resources, identifies specific action steps and time-tables and, finally, provides performance standards against which actual progress can be compared. It provides the template for the organization to develop.

Planning in the NHS

In this section I look at the areas in the NHS where planning is well established and at those areas where the art of planning is still relatively embryonic.

'An important aspect of market management is the ability to oversee the interaction of purchasers and providers and to spot gaps in service provision when they occur. The obverse is the need to avoid unnecessary duplication of services. In some cases purchasers will choose not to give priority to innovations in service provision which are desirable when seen from the perspective of the NHS as a whole. There must be capacity to fund these innovations in future.' (Ham, 1994)

Purpose of Plans

Planning healthcare in the NHS is complex, due to 'cross-boundary' issues. Liaison between different groups (eg Health

Authorities, Local Authorities, voluntary groups, fundholders, Trusts, patient representatives) is necessary to make the best use of the resources available.

In the NHS, which is naturally a highly political and bureaucratic organization, a good plan will provide a rational basis on which to gain approval for better resources. Increasingly it can be used to identify the most appropriate use for existing resources, where additional funding or support is not possible, or where the organization becomes a capitation loser under different funding formulae. The plan will assist the decision makers in identifying the key decisions for the enterprise and help systematic decision making with the best information available. The plan will also enable decision makers to find and implement solutions that are economically and politically feasible. Finally, the *process* of planning should involve all staff, as it is more likely to ensure their willingness to carry out the plan, and to ensure that analysis at grassroots level is incorporated.

'Planners ask, "How will next year be different?"
Winners ask "What must we do differently?"' (Hamel and Prahalad, 1989)

So, to be effective planners, it is not sufficient simply to map changes in the environment; we must also have good ideas about how the organization should respond to those changes.

CHECKLIST

The criteria below identify an effective plan. You can use this while writing the plan, to check against once it's been completed or against an existing plan that may be lying around, to see how well the organization did with its previous planning process.

- Is the plan concise enough yet long enough to give a clear understanding of what is intended?
- Does it have a purpose?
- Is there more than one course of action considered?

- Is the chosen course of action properly defined, and the reason for the choice understood?
- Does the plan show that the purpose can be attained?
- Are results expected from the chosen course of action specified?
- If the plan is to result in individual tasks are responsibilities allocated?

Keys to Growth

For some organizations growth is a realistic option for future development. If this is the case for your organization, then this list should help. If you are a provider, one of your concerns over the next couple of years may well be the prospect of merger with a neighbouring unit, to enhance the scope of services you provide, improve the quality, or for economies of scale. If you are a purchaser you may be considering how to work in a healthy alliance with other organizations to deliver better quality health-care services to your local population.

- Systematically seek out, find and reach for growth products and growth markets (for providers).
- Be self-critical about how good the current operations are, thereby presenting superior survival abilities.
- Top management should be composed of courageous, adventurous individuals who are driven by an energetic zeal to lead, but within financial guidelines.
- Establish formal processes of discovering opportunities and offsetting extreme risks through statements of the organization's goals. Aim at creativity.
- Establish through the chief executive an organizational environment of self-examination and effervescent high adventure.
- Accept that, even through the cautious practice of planning, there is still no guarantee of success; bad decisions may not be eliminated, but without planning it is still possible for some (but not many!) organizations to be successful.

This should provide you with some useful arguments to use with colleagues who are sceptical about the value of planning. These arguments may well need to be used time and again in order to convince people to get involved in the planning process.

However, even with all this preparation, we know that business planning will fail on some occasions. There could be one or more reasons for this, for example, where the chief executive does not believe in it and senior management does not exist; where the chief executive or chair allows no one but themselves to make decisions; where time cannot be found to write down plans or develop the strategy; where there is no desire to have better results than could have been achieved without planning; where there are hasty declarations of business objectives; where there is a lack of appreciation of the value of planning.

To help avoid this type of failure, here are some questions that you can ask to help get the plan right. These provide a useful checklist in planning meetings and get to the heart of making sure that the plan is relevant.

- What kind of structure does an organization need to perform its job effectively?
- What activities are necessary to achieve the purpose of the organization?
- What decisions will have to be made?
- What relationships are necessary between the people forming the structure?

Role of the Chief Executive

The attitude of the chief executive is crucial; they have overall responsibility for the organization, so it is in their interest for the plan to succeed. At the end of the day they are accountable for the appropriate use of NHS assets and resources. They must help to set demanding corporate goals and reshape the organization to fulfil the goals required. In this period of intense change for the NHS the chief executive should encourage an awareness of change in all aspects of the organizational environment; motivate cooperation, coordination, communication, collaboration and interdependence in all management roles; encourage the development of applicable strategies; monitor the effectiveness of these strategies and develop suitable management incentives.

Summary

In this chapter we have looked at the various activities that a healthcare manager can get involved in, both for the plan creation phase and for the plan implementation phase. Later chapters will go into these in more detail, but if you're asking yourself the question 'What can I contribute?' or 'How can I influence the process?' then here's a summary.

First, make sure your colleagues, particularly the person responsible for the planning process, know that you are willing and keen to participate. That way you'll be in a good position to influence the content of the plan. Use the checklists with colleagues to determine the value of the process and the content. This will be of particular help in planning meetings, where it is all too easy to get bogged down in detail or wander off the point.

An equally important role is to help the whole organization understand what the plan is and how its objectives are going to be achieved. By talking to colleagues not so immediately involved with the plan you'll start to get a picture of how well the organization has received the vision and is willing to live it. By addressing points of concern and sharing those with the planning team it will be possible to spot pitfalls early and take timely corrective action.

Chapter 2

The Planning Process

This chapter looks at all the steps in the planning process that an organization needs to go through; at the pitfalls and successes, using examples taken from around the UK. As a starting point, an organization needs a mission or vision that is meaningful to all staff and 'customers' in order to provide a sense of purpose.

The values that guide the organization are equally important, because they embody the ideals of the organization and offer a 'moral' or 'ethical' code that guides decision making within it. They are also valuable in communicating the reasons behind decisions should they be questioned (as, for example, in the case of Child B).

The next part of the process is a deep understanding of the environment. This includes social, technological, environmental and political factors that will influence the survival of the organization. Once the environment has been assessed, the plan will consider the strengths, weaknesses, opportunities and threats (SWOTs) for the organization, which result from the analysis. The next step in the process is consideration of key issues – those having a long-term and profound impact on the organization's success. Once these have been identified it is possible to consider the critical success factors that are areas of major importance for the organization.

From the critical success factors the objectives for the organization can be determined. Once SMART (specific, measurable, agreed (and actionable), realistic and timebound) objectives have been generated, then action plans can be developed, giving

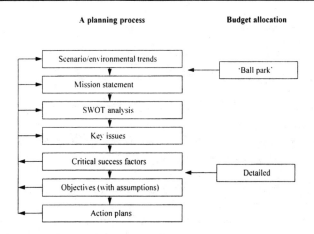

Figure 2.1 Stages in the planning process

responsibility for individuals to achieve activities within a given deadline.

How will this be achieved? Ideally, planning requires time away from day-to-day problems in order to take an overall view. In the NHS the culture of away days allows NHS managers to do just that.

The First Step – the Mission Statement

Each planning process will be different, depending on circumstances, but creating a mission statement is a useful place to start.

The mission statement is the *raison d'être* of the organization, together with an explicit statement of the values or philosophy guiding its work. It answers the question 'Why do we exist?', and is therefore a compelling vision that becomes the driving force of the organization. The mission statement:

- describes an organization's identity;
- states the strategic driving force of the organization (the focus);
- says what the organization is not;
- is cautiously optimistic (realistic and believable);
- arises from deeds and personal beliefs, not wishful hopes;
- avoids high-sounding and pious wording;

- is lucid and readily understandable;
- shows benefit to customers, employees, and owners;
- respects the distinguished history of the organization and gives meaning and achievement to the individual and the organization;
- includes values towards stakeholders, employees, managers, communities;
- is inspirational, answering the question 'Why would we be proud to work for this organization?'

Missions that are action oriented, innovative and responsive to competition provide staff with the sense of purpose and direction they need in times of rapid change. Simply having a vision is not enough; for it to be successful it must empower and be capable of implementation in a changing world.

Visionary organizations show resilience in the face of adversity and change and are likely to survive. For a commercial organization this means more than securing long-term financial returns. It must include a continuing and focused interest on the needs of its customers. In a public service it is more than an ability to survive changes in the environment. It is the active adoption of 'best practice' in meeting the needs of patients or clients.

Some mission statements have been attacked as being:

- vacuous, 'motherhood and apple pie' statements;
- a compromise between different parts of the organization trying to be all things to all people and therefore not fully reflecting any part of the organization;
- so visionary that they lose credibility, both with internal staff and the external audiences who the organization seeks to influence;
- inward looking and historical, rather than market or customer focused and future oriented;
- having no influence on *what* people do, or *how* they do it.

Creating a mission statement is often helpful, but only one of many steps towards building a visionary organization.

In order to create a mission statement the organization must step back and reflect on what it is trying to do. It needs to focus on the fundamental elements that define it and will make the difference between its success or failure.

CHECKLIST

Steps to creating a mission statement:

- Brainstorm – by pulling together people from within the organization, at all levels; set the scene by discussing the environment, challenges for the organization, the reasons for creating a mission statement, gazing into the future – where the organization expects to be in five or ten years' time.
- Clarify – by asking:
  - What do we want the organization to be and to stand for?
  - Where and how are we going to compete? What is our field of operation?
  - What do we want people in this organization to be good at? How do we want them to behave?
  - What do we have to be good at to succeed in our world?
- Validate – this is an ongoing process, checking internal consistency; the mission statement can then be drafted, bearing in mind succinctness, believability, motivational force, its impact (as opposed to its being broad and meaningless) and, above all, using plain language.
- Get feedback – from people other than in the brainstorming process.
- Continuously revisit – both the vision for the organization and the mission statement.

In this way, the foundations for a visionary organization can be laid down – ones that put the organization in a good position to survive and thrive in a rapidly changing environment.

The purpose of the NHS, which we see in most of the official documentation, is 'to secure through the resources available the greatest possible improvement in the physical and mental health of the people of England through four key measures':

1. By promoting good health.
2. By preventing ill health.
3. By diagnosing and treating injury and disease.
4. By caring for those with long term illness and disability.

Across the UK, NHS organizations will interpret the national purpose for their local communities. Here are some examples of mission statements:

'A clinical community providing first-class seamless care from home to hospital(s) to home.'

'The Authority's mission is:

(a) to help its population to become more health conscious and healthier; and
(b) to improve the quality of life for those suffering from ill health by investing in a continuous improvement of primary healthcare provision.'

Environmental Trends

Once the mission statement has been decided, the next step in the process is to look at the environment in which we operate as an organization. Understanding the trends that affect our environment can be a useful technique to start the planning process and help to identify likely elements that could influence the organization's strategy, such as economic factors, social, customer and competitive forces, technological change, regulatory and political environments, information technology and human resources.

By identifying and understanding the trends in the environment a realistic scenario can be developed which relates to the timescale of the plan. Given the current changing nature of the NHS, this is most likely to be of the order of 2–3 years. For example, current trends of particular importance to the NHS are changing demographics, a rise in consumerism and the continuing developments in medical technology.

Scenario

Part of the activity in studying environmental trends is constructing scenarios, based on different sorts of trends. A scenario is described as 'a consistent set of statements about possible future events and their dependencies, tracing the progression of the present to the future through a descriptive narrative.' It may feel like writing science fiction, based on events that have not happened yet, but it is a useful way of mapping out likely alternatives, together with some speculation about more extreme possibilities.

Scenario writing is a technique that emerged from managers realizing that the need to anticipate the future is an essential component in long-range planning (eg five years). It is an attempt to develop a picture of the future. You can write a range of scenarios and, after discussion, consensus can be reached with your colleagues on which is the most realistic option.

In identifying the trends within the environment and factors that can then be built into scenarios, it is helpful to group them together under a number of key headings. These are usefully described as a STEP analysis (Social, Technological, Economic and Political factors).

The following checklist of major factors and their possible impact on the future may prove valuable in your planning process.

CHECKLIST

Economic trends. Inflation and impact upon purchasing power of future customers; fiscal policy and its impact on government public spending; expenditure on infrastructure; exchange rates.

Demographics. Changes in birth-rate, life expectancy, age breakdown of society can have a significant impact upon marketing strategies of many organizations.

Changes in legal and quasi-legal regulations. Impact on marketing strategy can be important. Implications have to be predicted and evaluated.

Consumer lifestyle. Such changes can have considerable impact on product development, promotional strategies and channels of distribution.

Cost of commodities and raw materials (including the emergence of transnational cartels, like OPEC). Impact on cost of production; opening for substitution; market pressure for reduced consumption of more expensive materials.

National and international politics. Emergence of new markets; disappearance of traditional markets.

Technological changes. Impact on many aspects of organization's services and products.

Institutional developments. Such as changes in distribution channels; location of services.

Emerging media and communication channels. Such as interactive TV network system.

Social structure

Ecological/environmental lobbies and pressure groups. Affects processes; use of raw materials; location of services; acceptance by customers.

Information technology. Data communication; fund transfer; office automation; stock control; reordering procedures; logistics.

Infrastructure developments. Effect on local labour; change in catchment area demographics.

Changes in consumer attitudes to product/service contents. Need to consider changes in product/service strategies.

Changes in consumer habits (eg more sport and leisure; greater awareness of the value of outdoor activities). Important in assessing individuals' changing views in taking responsibility for their own health.

Biotechnology. Impact on medical developments can be significant.

Consumers' attitude to savings/spending. Significant in assessing risk management or co-payment strategies.

Where Are We Now?

Having established a mission statement for the organization and a 'most likely' scenario for the future (carefully making sure that it is not the rosy picture or the pessimistic view but is realistic), the SWOT analysis then allows us to consider the organization in relation to its competitors rather than the environment as a whole.

While an organization in the NHS may not have a strict competitor, as industry does, in practice all in the NHS are competing for public sector funding. Therefore, in order for projects/programmes to be supported, their advantages will need to be clearly demonstrated, to enable funders and line management to make comparisons with proposals and bids from other organizations.

The aim of the SWOT technique is 'to identify the extent to which the current strategy of an organization and its more specific strengths and weaknesses are relevant to, and capable of dealing with, the changes taking place in the environment'. So this looks at the really key points for the organization which make it different from its peers (colleagues or competitors). Key issues are identified as a result of the SWOT analysis, which are either controllable or uncontrollable by the organization. The controllable key issues that arise from the SWOT analysis are vital when we come to put the critical success factors into the plan. This is because these are the issues we *can* do something about.

The SWOT process involves identifying the strengths (internal) and weaknesses (internal) of the organization relative to any competitors, and assessing these against the opportunities (external) and threats (external) in the environment. A key question to answer before embarking on a SWOT analysis is 'Who do you consider your competitors to be?'

Once again, it's not easy for a public service to answer this question. Suggestions from organizations I have worked with include other purchasers, other providers or, indeed, others competing for the same resources (that could mean local authorities, academic institutions or, more widely, housing, environment, defence and all the other demands on the public purse).

How is a SWOT Constructed?

Strengths

As mentioned before, these are internal to the organization and are abilities that give an advantage over competitors, ie the things that the organization is good at and does better than competitors. They are therefore key *differences* between the organization and its competitors.

Weaknesses

These are also internal to the organization and are situations, problems or obstacles that the organization has and its competitors do not.

Opportunities

These are external developments that could enhance the organization's future position if taken advantage of. You can use them to determine basic directions for growth and service development, either in commissioning or provision of services. Correctly identifying good opportunities can sometimes mean the difference between future survival and organizational decay.

Threats

These are external developments (present or future) that could seriously affect the organization's future adversely. These also need watching and dealing with, wherever possible.

Below is a useful format in which to consider a SWOT.

SWOT ANALYSIS

Strengths	Weaknesses
Opportunities	Threats

In addition to the SWOT, a summary of reasons for bad or good performance of the organization is useful at this stage. It should be a concise, interesting analysis of the environment. When added to the business plan it provides the reader with an anchor point on which to base the developments laid out later on.

In writing down the SWOT, each component needs to be prioritized and the five most important listed in each category. However, it is worth remembering that, in today's fast moving environment, today's strengths can become tomorrow's weaknesses, and vice versa. You need to review the analysis regularly to ensure the proposed plan is still workable.

Key Questions for the SWOT

In constructing a SWOT for the organization, one could consider:

Internal factors

- Which healthcare services are we best at?
- What are our outputs?
- What structure do we, and should we, have (jobs, organization, function)?
- What internal and external communication systems do we have?
- What opportunities are there for new and/or improved services?
- What human resources do we need (numbers, skills, attitudes and behaviours)?
- What is our financial strength (reserves, cashflow, margins)?
- What is our reputation (within the health service or the outside world)?
- What volatility do we have (eg staff turnover)?
- What is the cohesiveness between strategies?
- What is our marketing ability?
- What is our match of organizational capability to deliver key aims and objectives?
- What information systems do we have?

External factors

- What changes in national or local politics may affect our service? Can these be anticipated?

- Are there economic factors that may affect our ability to meet objectives (eg cash limits in the NHS, development of competitors for contracts or staff in the area)?
- Have we allowed for changing customer and client expectations?
- Have we taken into account, as far as possible, the strengths and weaknesses of any competitors?

By considering these areas it should be possible to identify key differences between the organization and its competitors. In order to make this a meaningful exercise it would be useful to have a list of the organization's 'stakeholders' and to determine what measures of success would be appropriate for these stakeholder groups. We look at stakeholders in Chapter 7.

Remember that the SW part of the SWOT has an internal focus, and that the OT part is an external perspective.

Here is an example of a SWOT that has been condensed from a long list of considerations to a priority list by an organization that has gone through the SWOT activity in small management groups. It is a good discipline to prioritize at each stage of the planning process and, in addition, justify the priorities, which will provide the justification of the plan when complete.

Doing the SWOT in small groups generates a more comprehensive list than asking individuals to go away and think of their own list. There will, of course, be some common threads that different groups will all include. These will give a clue as to what the most important areas are likely to be – but don't discount ideas that only appear in one group – they can still be critical in deciding what to do.

Strengths

1. Motivated, committed, enthusiastic staff.
2. Management information system in place.
3. Healthy alliances, eg joint appointments.
4. Broad range of background experience.

Weaknesses

1. Few shared care guidelines developed.
2. Not knowing the health needs of the local population.

3. Lack of role clarity in the management team.
4. Lack of focus on healthcare outputs among GPs.
5. Duplicated/overlapping services by providers – unnecessary waste.

Opportunities

1. GP fundholding and commissioning groups.
2. Primary care led NHS (seamless service).
3. Health of the nation/health gain/functional independence for resident population.
4. Increased public awareness of health matters.
5. Medical and clinical audit.

Threats

1. Prioritization of national vs local priorities.
2. Inflexibility of national GP contract.
3. Unnecessary competition between (purchasing) authorities serving the same population.
4. Unfair competition between providers to attract lucrative, rather than essential, services.
5. Pace of change in NHS.

Do some of these look familiar? If so, be reassured to know that others in the NHS are experiencing the same issues. However, I do not claim that the above list is the one for all NHS organizations – there may be other factors in your area that need attention. And, of course, the strategy and plans for dealing with them may be very different.

Key Issues

From an analysis of the environment a number of *key issues* can be determined. You can recognize which these are because these will have a high impact on your organization's future. Some of these will be outside the organization's control. Where that is the case, you need only to keep monitoring them over time. If their status changes and they become controllable then they will require critical success factors. Other key issues will be controllable and it is on these that you should focus your efforts. Key issues should be expressed in the plan as statements or questions, not just stab points, otherwise you may end up with simply listing out the SWOT again. Statements or, more easily, questions will mean that the answers to the questions (the critical success factors) will be more straightforward to define. Key issues, above all, are areas of major importance and demand top management attention.

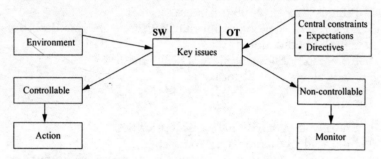

Figure 2.2 Key issues

For example, a purchasing group may consider a key issue to be how to balance the requirements of the national health policy agenda with the needs of the local population. I look at this particular area in a Chapter 5. It is likely that, having assessed the SWOT, you will have a handful of key issues which demand action. Again, the list of key issues should not be too long in order to be manageable and, ideally, it should be prioritized. If the list *is* too long, it will prove more difficult to address, given your resources.

Managerial Dilemmas

There are a number of critical questions with which both purchasers and providers are wrestling in today's changing NHS.

- How are we to handle the intense pressure from politicians to deliver more for less?
- How are we to cope with the public's rising expectations?
- How can we respond to growing health inequalities within our communities?

These questions are likely to be common to many NHS organizations around the country, and refer directly to the key drivers of change in the NHS – rising consumerism, changing demographics and the ever-present political pressures.

Other key questions that could usefully be asked are:

- Should certain services be excluded altogether?
- What is the role of the Health Authority or Board in relation to the role of doctors (particularly with the advent of total fundholding pilots)?
- Do clinical guidelines and protocols offer the best way forward?

Here is an example of how a key issue that came out of the opportunity 'Encourage GP focus on healthcare outputs' from our earlier SWOT list might be expressed: 'How can we ensure a balanced approach to value within cost constraints among GPs?'

The key issue identifies that GPs see patients as individuals and not as a practice population; that the GPs in this area view the NHS reforms as a cost-cutting exercise, rather than a platform to achieve health gain; and that, currently, GPs here (and, possibly, more widely) have little information about the effectiveness or efficacy of the services that they provide or commission. This leads us neatly to the next step of the process – creating the critical success factors.

Critical Success Factors

The organization obviously needs to do something about those key issues over which it has a degree of control. These can be formulated as a number of critical success factors, which provide a list of statements on areas in which the organization must excel in order to operate successfully and achieve its objectives – so they are considered major decision areas. The statements are best expressed as positive, action-oriented statements, answering the questions posed by the key issues. It is important not to be vague – we need to recognize whether it is done or not!

Achieving success is a question of balancing what both the present and future require. So, while an organization is spending time and resources on today's priorities (concentrating on doing better what it does today), it must also spend time and resources on building tomorrow (concentrating on doing something different tomorrow). Bearing this in mind will make creating the critical success factor statements easier.

Questions to help in defining critical success factors include:

- What do you need to do as a group to succeed with the regional office?
- What are you employed to do?
- What must you do to prevent a take-over?
- What is critical for your survival as a group?

If we look at the key issue we described on page 25 one or more critical success factors may fall out of it, eg we must support GPs to include a broad health economics approach when planning their activity.

Let us look at critical success factors that have been devised for the NHS as a whole. These are included in the Planning and Priorities Guidance for the NHS 1996/97, which contains six national medium-term priorities, supported by six baseline requirements and objectives for purchasers. These are the basic standards 'which every NHS purchaser knows they are expected to meet by virtue of being part of the NHS'. These are the NHS's 'must do's. They are:

1. Progress towards Health of the Nation targets.
2. Patients' Charter standards and guarantees.
3. Waiting list targets and guarantees.
4. National and local efficiency targets.
5. Agreed financial and activity targets.
6. Control of drugs expenditure.

In addition, the selection of national priorities has been based on two stated themes, both of which are considered critical success factors for the NHS as a whole:

- Moving the focus away from organization structure towards improving health and the quality of care.
- The need to reinforce and realize the commitment in the NHS to partnership, collaboration and teamwork.

Where Do We Want to Get to?

Moving on from the question 'Where are we now?', and following on from critical success factors, the organization is ready to consider 'Where do we want to get to?' – its objectives.

Objectives

These should be SMART statements (see page 12) – to be achieved within a given timeframe and resulting from the pursuit of a particular strategy. The statement can be qualitative or quantitative and should have sufficient meaning to enable recognition of when it has been achieved.

Objectives should also be costed, where appropriate; be robust for all the likely scenarios and consider the 'market' (in NHS terms, the patient and their expectations from the service).

In describing an objective, it is helpful to start the statement with 'To...', which will make it very clear that you are looking to do something proactive in dealing with your environment. For example, you might think about the critical success factor we looked at on page 26, from which a number of objectives might emerge, such as, 'To ensure that all GPs are able to measure healthcare outputs by the start of the next financial year'. By doing this you start to define the work plan for the organization, which helps when we move on to the next stage – that of devising the action plans.

Having set the objectives, it is important to list the assumptions against which they were set. The assumptions are an important part of the subsequent review process to see the rate of progress towards the achievement of the objectives (see Chapter 4). They define the conditions under which you, and the organization, are able to deliver the objectives. Any change in the conditions affects the organization's ability to achieve the objectives set and agreed.

Example of Objectives from Planning and Priorities Guidance 1996/97

The priorities listed are:

(a) To work towards the development of a primary care led NHS, in which decisions about the purchasing and provision of healthcare are taken as close to patients as possible.
(b) In partnership with local authorities, to purchase and monitor a comprehensive range of secure, residential, in-patient and community services to enable people with mental illness to receive effective care and treatment in the most appropriate setting in accordance with their needs.
(c) Improve the cost effectiveness of services throughout the NHS, and thereby secure the greatest health gain from the resources available, through formulating decisions on the basis of appropriate evidence about clinical effectiveness.
(d) Give greater voice and influence to users of NHS services and their carers in their own care, the development and definition of standards set for NHS services locally and the development of NHS policy both locally and nationally.
(e) Ensure, in collaboration with local authorities and other organizations, that integrated services are in place to meet needs for continuing healthcare and allow elderly, disabled or vulnerable people to be supported in the community.
(f) Develop NHS organizations as good employers with particular reference to workforce planning, education and training, employment policy and practices, the development of teamwork, reward systems, staff utilization and staff welfare.

Objectives for Health Authorities and Boards could be:

- To improve the health and healthcare of the population.
- To devise acceptable measures of health gain (outcome/effectiveness).
- To provide leadership on health issues.
- To devise realistic ways for involving people in providing information to assist in improving the health of the population, including:
  - health needs analysis;

- priority setting and resource allocation processes;
- health promotion activities;
- review of quality and type of services.
• To ensure that individuals are satisfied with the services delivered.
• To be sensitive to individual and group needs when taking decisions at population level.

For providers, it is likely that the following would be considered key objectives:

• To provide an effective and efficient service.
• To eliminate unnecessary investigations.
• To maximize the use of new technology.
• To provide guidelines for best clinical practice for a variety of conditions.

These are objectives to which both management and clinicians would agree.

In checking through the objectives you generate, some helpful questions are:

• How realistic is this for you?
• How will this be measured?
• When should this be done by?

If quarter ends are used as timescales it is important to check that not all objectives are scheduled to be met at the same time, but prioritized to be spread more evenly through the year. That way, the organization is less likely to move from one bureaucratic crisis to another, which takes up a lot of time, spent in a relatively unproductive way.

How Do We Get There?

Action Plans

Once objectives have been set, the action plans for each can be devised. The action plan is a list of inputs or activities, together with associated responsibilities, accountabilities and timescales, demonstrating how you intend to achieve each objective. The action plan assigns individual responsibilities and so can be used to set work plans for each department or member of staff in the organization. It also contains the costings associated with each action. These costs, when aggregated, are the budget for the organization, needed to undertake the plan.

The Management Approach

The process associated with action plans can be broken down into seven steps.

1. Agree objectives and set targets with all those who will be responsible for achieving them. For example, which innovations in patient management are necessary? The targets set should, of course, be SMART (see page 12).
2. List all tasks and actions.
3. Agree individual responsibilities. It is helpful to appoint a 'champion' to coordinate and oversee the project (see Chapters 6 and 7).
4. Identify additional skills and resources (money, people, time).
5. Set a timetable. This should be realistic. It helps to maintain momentum and sets goals towards which individuals can work.
6. Monitor and review progress. Keep records of each step and produce an action list (eg a wall planner) to remind team members of their responsibilities. Hold regular meetings to review progress and identify/resolve difficulties.
7. Formal review and celebration. Build in a formal review at the end of the timetable to assess the impact of the innovation, celebrate the success of the project and recognize the achievement of individuals in making it work.

It is helpful to set out action plans in the following way.

Objective:

Action Plan (To do list)

What   By whom   By when   How much (resources)

So, for the objective we set on page 27 a number of action plans would fall out, eg:

- GPs to receive postgraduate training in health economics over the next 12 months.
- Public health to brief GPs on local health needs and effective strategies for intervention.
- Consultants and GPs to agree shared guidelines for patient management to address specific health needs.

The Budget and the Business Plan

We mentioned earlier that assigning costs to the action plans will give the organization some idea of the resources needed to deliver the requirements of the business plan. This is very much a bottom-up process. In parallel with that, it is useful to do the top-down exercise, based on the allocation to the Authority or Board; or, for providers, to plan from the previous year's actual spend.

Analysis of resources for a purchaser

Money allocated to healthcare contracts
ECRs
Administration
Legal liability
Joint finance
Earmarked funds
NHS R&D

In this way, purchasers will be able to determine whether the allocation is sufficient to cover all their requirements, or whether adjustments will need to be made.

Budget headings for providers

Staff
Equipment
Consumables/supplies
Overheads (estates, support services, management)
Capital charges

Capital projects
Cost improvement programme
NHS R&D

Providers must ensure they meet the financial requirements of Trust status:

- secure a 6 per cent return on net assets;
- break even on income and expenditure (after paying interest and public dividend capital);
- meet its external financial limit.

In an ideal world, the top-down allocations and the bottom-up aggregation will match, if not exactly, then within 1 or 2 per cent. The next step in the process is one of reconciliation and adjustment. Once that has been established, the top management team can be fairly confident that the plan is workable.

CHECKLISTS FOR PURCHASERS AND PROVIDERS

Purchasers
How does the budget:

- reflect the efficiency gains?
- absorb the policy shifts (eg increase in day cases)?
- allow for ECRs?
- profile case-mix?
- show developments (eg effective new treatments)?
- show the impact of GP fundholders?
- clarify the organization of the business?
- enable meaningful monitoring?
- show economic profiling, based on needs?
- get derived (eg zero-based planning, prioritizing or needs based)?

Providers
How does the budget:

- show the income streams?
- show the percentage of risk income and the degree of risk?
- get derived (eg zero-based budgeting, income stream or historical)?
- reflect the organization of the business (eg by clinical directorate and/or activity)?
- show increases in productivity?
- show policy changes?
- describe business case developments?
- show loss or gain of business and its impact through sensitivity analysis?

The Management Process

Of course, simply writing the plan is not the end of the process. A business plan should not be formed in isolation. It should have measures against which the organization's progress can be checked and the plan should be continually reviewed. This is part of the process where the Board can play a useful role (see Chapter 9).

Using plans as standards for measuring managerial performance means that they become part of the fabric of the organization and not a one-off exercise that is not relevant to your future activities.

Contingency Planning

Although the business plan will be written to deal with the most likely future situation in mind, a good plan also includes a section that tries to answer the question 'What if...?'

The contingency plan is therefore also a key part of the process and is particularly useful for the NHS. It's a way of trying to minimize the impact of surprises (nice or nasty). So, for example, how would your organization react to the following 'What ifs?'

'What if we are asked to deliver a 5 per cent efficiency gain, rather than 3 per cent?'

'What if we are asked to make a headcount reduction of 10 per cent over the next two years?'

'What if we are successful in our bid for additional funding and receive £1 million?'

It's easy to say 'Well we'll think about that if it happens', but the best organizations have an idea in advance, which allows them to take prompt action when the seemingly unexpected occurs.

Techniques to Assist the Planning Process

There are a number of techniques that have been used successfully by both commercial and public sector organizations to help in generating their business plans.

Brainstorming

The idea behind brainstorming is that a group of people come together and, as a group, think of as many ideas as possible, either new activities for the organization or to solve a problem. It is of most benefit in situations where there are many possible answers, rather than only one or two suitable ones. The environment for brainstorming is one in which no idea is evaluated or judged – that comes later, in a sifting process, which will discard the unworkable. Edward de Bono, a leading authority in the field of creative and lateral thinking, describes this creative process as 'green hat' thinking and the process of using judgement as 'black hat' thinking.

The group should have a 'leader' or chair to organize the event, keep the session creative and under control. Their role is *not* to manage the group members, other than to prevent any judgemental or evaluative comments. It is also necessary to have a 'scribe' – someone to write down all the ideas that the group generates. It is important that this person writes what the group members say, rather than their interpretation of what is said. *All* ideas, however strange, should be captured. A good number for a brainstorming session is between six and ten participants.

The brainstorming session should start by getting the participants warmed up – often this works by doing a 'dummy' brainstorm. In this way participants who have not brainstormed before can become familiar with the idea of contributing ideas and will learn not to comment on others' ideas. A simple one could be 'a new use for paper cups'.

Not much time is needed for an effective brainstorm, often only about 20 minutes after the preparation and briefing parts of the process, during which time approaching 200 ideas can be generated. Further ideas may occur to participants afterwards, so it's a good idea to circulate the outputs from the session for people to add any new ideas they have had.

Evaluation

Once the ideas from the brainstorming session have been collated it helps to wait a few days before evaluating them. A list of criteria for the evaluation needs to be drawn up, which all the ideas will be vetted against. The success criteria suggested on pages 44–6 may be helpful in defining what these should be. The ideas can then be mapped out, either in a matrix (eg an axis describing consistency with the organization's mission and a second axis that covers feasibility) or in a table, where each option is awarded points against weighted criteria (eg health gain, cost effectiveness, acceptability with local population, consistency with national and local priorities). This latter technique is the one we see often in a *Which?* evaluation of consumer goods. Evaluation is where the 'black hat' thinking is applied; logical negative, judgement and caution are the key factors here. This process (combining brainstorming and evaluation) can be helpful in choosing an appropriate direction for the organization, or in deciding between a number of different possible courses of action.

Chapter 3

Implementation

This chapter will explore why plans fail and how to reduce the chances of failure.

The Challenge of Implementation

> 'The business plan must be realistic and fundable, and used as a working document and, importantly, it must be management's, and not an outsider's. Once the plan is drafted, implementation then presents the real challenge.' (Deffenbaugh, 1990)

So, the planning process is a systematic and rational way to generate an argument for more money, resources, or agreement to the direction of the authority. However, plans do fail, generally not in the creation phase, but in the implementation phase, which is why we are now going to look at monitoring, corrective action and review.

How Do We Get There? (continued)

We are still at this stage trying to answer the question 'How do we get there?', but at this point we are moving from a paper exercise into the workload planned for the organization. Implementation is, arguably, the most important part of the plan. The plan must be implemented, otherwise the time invested in putting it together has been entirely wasted. Working on getting there and checking on how we are doing are a major part of the plan's implementation. Monitoring progress towards the achievement of the plan is straightforward when action plans have been developed. The other point to bear in mind here is that we are also looking at how to do things better. This means that learning is the most important part of this activity.

For an organization to be successful in a fast changing environment, such as the 1990s, it needs to be:

- customer responsive/focused;
- integrated;
- able to devolve decision making/less hierarchical;
- effective in its use of resources;
- fast acting;
- continually adapting to its customers' needs.

In order to achieve this, it is likely that those working within the organization would need to change some of their working practices and behaviours. In this chapter we will address both organizational change and personal change; for the latter we will use a framework of competencies.

If your organization is to survive, it is likely that you will identify appropriate times at which any corrective actions required must be agreed. Involvement, communication and positive thinking are critical. Leaving people in the dark makes it more difficult to get their cooperation when trying to change the goal posts or, worse, the rules of the game. No plans are etched in stone, and so they will need to be modified according to changing circumstances. Planning will not give a perfect crystal ball; nor will it enable prediction of the future with extreme accuracy. However, changing circumstances may mean that you activate the contingency plan, because that is the new combination of circumstances within which you are operating.

A good plan should result in the integration of the organization's activities and will encourage your best efforts towards the attainment of corporate goals. Planning will not necessarily prevent you, or an organization, from making mistakes, but seeks to minimize the impact those mistakes may have.

As I mentioned before, it is also necessary to keep the organization informed and involved. Therefore communication is important. It should be repetitive, two-way and be used to share both the plan and its results. Having the plan at least provides a common language for you and your colleagues and staff.

In persuading people of the importance of planning, it is useful to remember that its value is to coordinate planning for scarce resources – capital, manpower, facilities. It helps us to develop a clearer idea of priorities and objectives – scope of activities, size, rate of growth, and the economic and social priorities. It enables the organization to produce more explicit policies for debate with stakeholders – government, trade unions, the public, special interest groups, etc.

It enables the organization to involve more staff in discussion about the future – to provide a basis for better decisions, to encourage innovation and initiative, and to improve motivation and morale. It also enables the organization to survive and grow and to achieve other financial and social goals in a rapidly changing environment.

We have to assume, therefore, that we are working in a changing environment – a pretty reasonable assumption for the NHS in the 1990s. There are probably a number of different approaches that could be taken to ensure longer-term survival, so it is worth spending some time looking at this.

Questions that are helpful to assess change strategies are:

- Has it been tried before?
- Are we ready for change?
- Who makes the decisions?
- Who are the key people?
- Who might support the change?
- Who might be against the change?
- Where do I go next?

If you come up with positive answers to the above questions, then the change can be managed. The whole process is quite straightforward – the difficult part is in changing behaviour, as we will see.

The Change Process

In order to implement change, there are a number of steps to go through.

1. Agree the key aims and objectives of the proposed change.
2. Explore ways of implementing the change.
3. Identify all the necessary tasks and agree individual responsibilities.
4. Agree a realistic timetable.
5. Review progress regularly.
6. Celebrate success.
7. Agree future actions needed to achieve continuous improvement.

So far, so good. We have explored the process of managing organizational change. Now let's look at change for individuals.

Competencies for Managing Change

I mentioned earlier that by far the most difficult part of the change process is changing the behaviour of individuals – we all dislike change and are usually happiest when working in a familiar environment, with well-accepted and understood rules. So, in order to manage change, somehow people need to be persuaded that it is a 'good thing'. There is a technique that is now being encouraged in both commercial and public service organizations – that of looking at competencies.

A competency framework describes the skills, knowledge and behaviour that are required by the people throughout an organization to achieve both positive performance of day-to-day activity, but also to move the organization forward and make it capable of surviving in the future. There are a number of competencies that will affect an organization's or individual's ability to change. These can be considered as an iceberg, with skills and knowledge as the aspects that are above the surface and the most visible of the requirements. A number of underlying elements of competencies are less visible, but they direct and control the surface behaviour. These are social role and self-image, which exist at a conscious level; and traits and motives below the surface, lying closer to the person's core, at the subconscious level.

The value of competency assessments is in determining the best mix of skills and individuals to tackle the issues of the day and for the future. One trend that is common in both the commercial and public sectors is that many organizations are 'delayering'. This results in fewer opportunities for upward promotion and an increase in scope for the remaining jobs. In this environment advancement comes from broadening skills, knowledge and behaviour to the benefit of both the individual and the organization. A competency framework can act as a 'route map' for that development.

Core Competency Framework

The core competency framework can be divided into a number of key areas. The ones we use at Glaxo Wellcome are:

1. Personal qualities: personal accountability, personal organization, self-development, creativity and innovation, flexibility and continuous improvement.
2. Planning to achieve: gathering, analysing and interpreting data to produce information, problem solving and decision making, establishing a plan, implementing and monitoring achievement.
3. Business and customer focus: this covers the organization's environment, business environment and customer focus.
4. Supportive leadership: this looks at effective leadership and empowerment.
5. Working with others: the last in the list that looks at teamworking, managing conflict and being supportive, developing colleagues, giving and receiving feedback, networking and building relationships and, above all, communication.

While your list may be different, the one above provides a useful starting point in identifying what your organization needs from its staff.

Communication

When we looked at communication earlier we concentrated on communications from the organization to stakeholders. Communication is also a core competency for individuals, in working with others. In my organization it is described as delivering clear, concise messages using appropriate media. A person exhibiting exemplary communication would have excellent spoken, written and presentation skills; listens to others and conveys clear and simple messages verbally; is calm; open and non-judgemental; asks questions; writes clearly and concisely; presents in a professional manner, having researched the subject thoroughly; tailors the message to the audience; manages own IT; uses appropriate communications channels quickly and easily.

Communication is the process of making relevant information freely available to the appropriate people.

COMMUNICATIONS CHECKLIST

- What action do I want?
- What is the main aim or purpose of the communication?
- Who will receive it?
- How is the recipient likely to react?
- How much will they need to know?
- Is my timing right?
- What is the main subject?
- Are the major points clear?
- Are the tone and language appropriate?
- Is the action required clear?
- Does the recipient know what is expected of him or her?
- Is there any ambiguity?
- Have the facts been checked?
- Will I need to follow it up?
- What is the best medium for communication – memo, telephone, face to face?
- Will this communication encourage people to challenge the status quo?
- Have any new ideas come up as a result of this communication?
- Will the time spent on the communication be well spent?

Chapter 4

Evaluation

In this chapter we look in detail at techniques for evaluating the success of plans.

How Far Have We Got?

This is a question frequently asked in all organizations and can be answered more quickly and easily if the measures for success have been identified within the original plan.

Management by Objectives

A common technique to assist with evaluation is management by objectives (MBO). This looks at the improvement of performance by providing the means with which each manager can monitor and help improve his or her standard.

Management by objectives requires certain basic steps on the part of management, and must include:

- reviewing critically and restating the organization's strategic and tactical plans;
- clarifying with each manager their key results and performance standards and gaining contribution and commitment to these; the relationship between each manager must be understood, so that teamwork is made easier;
- establishing rigorous procedures for control and self-control of

progress; this will always consider performance and potential review;
- establishing imaginative management development programmes, including training plans, selection, salary and succession plans;
- providing conditions in which these results can be achieved; this means a supportive climate of opinion, effective organization structure and sound management control information.

Problems can be encountered when applying MBO principles. Employees may distrust the process itself or what it is designed to achieve. Management may resent the introduction of a prescriptive monitoring tool. The commitment needed to follow through, eg with written assessments and the time taken to complete this may be problematic for management. There is a need for management to set valid objectives, which may in turn be hampered by a lack of relevant and useful data. Above all, there is a need for top management backing, which may not exist in every case.

However, by implementing an MBO process, an organization would be able to measure the effectiveness of its introduction by looking at a number of indicators, eg the ratio of internal placements to external appointments, a rise in internal management standards with a more professional approach, better organization structures, more accountability within the structure and more emphasis on training for specific performance improvement.

In a health service context, there are some obviously useful measures for checking on the organization's progress against plan.

Monitoring Results

'Measures of health, illness, and patient satisfaction are essential to the establishment of needs for, and outcomes of, health care.' (Wilkin *et al*, 1992)

Monitoring results is not the end of the process for business planning. It is just part of the process for continuous improvement, which seeks, in the health service setting, to meet the health needs of the population in the most effective way possible.

There are three questions which are helpful to ask at this point.

1. How is the quality of the health services provided measured, and how are the ones offering value for money identified?
2. How are areas for investment and disinvestment decided?
3. How is the impact of proposed changes measured?

The NHS has historically been good at measuring the activities of the people within it, through finished consultant episodes, patient consultations with GPs, numbers of prescriptions, etc. It has also been very good at identifying new areas for development, or where investments in services could be made. As a consequence, particularly in recent years, the NHS has responded well to a number of environmental pressures – demographic trends, technological advance and increasing public expectations. The response has been measured in terms of NHS expenditure, which has increased, in real terms, year on year throughout the life of the current government; and in Patients' Charter targets, which have shown more patients treated by the service, reductions in waiting times, etc.

Despite these positive indicators, what evidence is there that these increased activities and funds have resulted in either improved health for the population or improved quality of healthcare services for patients?

Measures of Success

One way in which the NHS has tried to answer this question is by measuring progress against the Health of the Nation targets, looking at the results of what the NHS is doing for the population, in partnership with other agencies.

In order to conduct an appropriate evaluation of services, it is crucial to generate meaningful measures of success. In broad terms, these can be different for different groups – patients, GPs, Health Authorities and Trusts.

Trusts
First, let us look at results from the Trust's perspective. These can be absolute or discretionary.

- improving health of patients and staff;
- improving outcomes;
- improved quality of services;

- consumer satisfaction;
- survival of Trust;
- growth of Trust (market share/range of services provided);
- value for money;
- financial stability/not making a loss;
- staff/professional needs satisfied;
- consumer satisfaction (GPFH and HA);
- investment in newer technology.

A number of critical success factors can be associated with this list, such as good communication (for example, the population says the service provided by the Trust is the best locally available); forward planning is also essential to maintain this successful position over the long term.

GPs
Measures of success here could include:

- speedy access to other services;
- healthy patients;
- satisfied patients;
- level of reconsultations;
- good communications with other providers;
- choice for patients that GPs can exercise;
- involvement in purchasing decisions;
- increase of patient list;
- degree of autonomy;
- funding for practice staff/premises;
- keeping within budget (if fundholders);
- above target net income;
- lack of complaints to GMC;
- increased range of services provided (to increase income);
- staff morale;
- own morale/family relationships;
- no night call responsibility;
- professional development;
- patient suggestions;
- easy ECRs;
- good social services support;
- less bureaucracy ('Patients not Paper').

Health Authorities
These suggestions are based on the role of Health Authorities in generating strategy, supporting providers and monitoring service standards.

- rates of reconsultation;
- purchase within budget;
- reaching Health of the Nation targets and local targets;
- meeting Patients' Charter targets;
- business plan on target (timings, budgets, etc);
- improving mortality rates (ie decreasing);
- agreed strategy working with providers and GPs;
- maintaining relationships with all providers;
- effective working with contractors;
- effective consultation with public;
- high staff morale;
- adequate premises;
- smooth handling of problems – low media interest, or effective media management;
- avoiding bad press/headlines;
- choice and variety of service for patients.

Patients
This could be the most important group to canvass opinions from. There is probably less reliance on the technical perfection of the activity carried out, and more on the perception the patient or carer has of the overall service provided.

- increased quality of life, eg mobility, by patients' own measures;
- increased patient/public health literacy, eg better understanding of process and realistic expectations;
- knowledge of short- and long-term outcomes;
- taking control of their own health, empowerment;
- ready and immediate access to healthcare services;
- confidence in provider;
- information about quality of service provided;
- short wait for in-patient or out-patient appointment.

The Concept of Outcomes

The definition of an outcome is a 'real or visible effect'.

If an organization is concerned with outcomes it is involved with the causal relationships between a sequence of conditions or events. In a health service context, outcomes can be positive or negative, ranging from complete health to death. Outcomes should be concerned with the total physical and mental well-being of the patient and not measured solely in terms of clinical efficacy.

For example, many studies of cancer treatments have focused solely on survival rates, regardless of the quality of life experienced by patients and their relatives. Much medical and clinical audit has stopped short of recording information on the extent to which patients' needs are met and where desirable outcomes have been achieved. So there is scope for improvement in how these important activities are measured – this could well be a suitable topic for a quality initiative.

In 1958 WHO described health as 'A state of complete physical, mental and social well-being, and not merely the absence of disease or infirmity.' So, in this sense, positive health can be seen as patients achieving functional excellence. This is, then, a helpful definition for managers and clinicians in considering the impact of existing services and in judging proposals for change.

Looking at the patterns of service delivery is as important as evaluating the clinical interventions employed and can just as usefully serve as a topic of study for audit. I look at the value of audit in the next chapter.

From what has been covered so far it seems easy to measure healthcare inputs such as people, equipment and medicines. However, simply measuring these elements in isolation will not provide a fair indication of the worth of that input. For example, the cost of medicines in the treatment of a particular disease is relatively easy to calculate. The cost of providing secondary care is also becoming easier to measure, due to the contracting process within the NHS (see Chapter 8).

Much harder to measure is the cost and outcome of disease prevention or health promotion in any given disease area (eg the cost of running an anti-smoking campaign in schools, nursing and ancillary services in chemotherapy, or the effects of failing to control emesis which occurs as a result of cancer or surgical treatment with anaesthetics). However, all these additional costs have a role to play in treating a condition and some assessment is needed of the relative value of *every* element of the treatment process (see programme budgeting on page 84).

Figure 4.1 shows how timely and appropriate interventions with medicines at the primary care stage can lead to savings in secondary care costs (surgery, rehabilitation, nursing, etc). The actual cost benefits can also be accompanied by significant patient benefits (in terms of pain, distress, lost work, etc). However, as stated earlier, this audit activity will not be effective

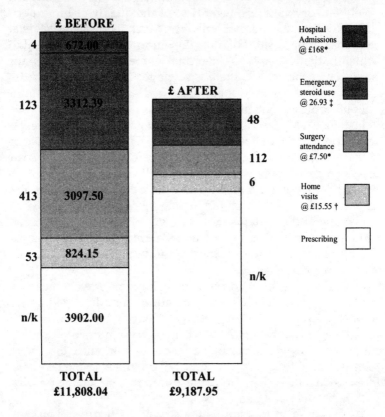

* Sources: Health Service costing return 1987 DHSS, NAHAT 1990, OHE compendium 1993
† Calculated on basis of equivalent to lower rate night visit fee *nb this may not reflect accurate true cost*
‡ Calculated on basis of fee for emergency treatment (£20.95) plus average prescription cost

Figure 4.1 Effects of an asthma clinic on costs and outcomes

if the criteria for measurement are not robust in the first place. The list of quality markers in Chapter 5 (p.67) provides a comprehensive guide to the areas which can be usefully:

(a) incorporated into corporate contracts;
(b) incorporated into contracts between purchasers and providers (see Chapter 8);
(c) used as measures for audit purposes;
(d) used in comparison of different providers;
(e) used in comparison of different purchasers;
(f) used to identify improvements in the quality of services provided as part of CQI/TQM initiatives.

In looking at what sorts of outcomes to measure, healthcare systems have always had difficulty in linking cause and effect. So even if there are improved outcomes for patients, given the many processes which contribute to the care of the patient it is difficult to link one specific intervention or treatment as the causative factor. Nevertheless, by measuring both outcomes and recording the processes used to get there, the Health Service is in a better position to justify the decisions it takes. The practical measures mentioned in the list of quality markers include quality of life, health-related quality of life, satisfaction with healthcare and process-based measures.

The practical limitations of measuring the effect of health services include:

• the problem of several treatments taking place simultaneously;
• the start and end of treatments are often unclear, eg long courses of rehabilitation or continuous symptom control in chronic conditions;
• the treatment has a low level effect which is difficult to measure to determine its significance in contributing to the outcome.

However, if we do make an attempt to measure the effects, what instruments are available to be used, and when is the most appropriate situation for each?

The measures and tools shown in Figure 4.2 go some way to answering the first of the questions posed earlier, 'How is the quality of services provided measured?' To complete the answer to this question and to answer the second ('How are areas for

QUANTITY OF LIFE	PROCESS BASED OUTCOME	QUALITY OF LIFE Health-related quality of life Dimensions of health			SATISFACTION WITH HEALTH CARE
		Physical	Social	Mental	
Mortality					Patient satisfaction surveys
Avoidable premature mortality	Re-admission rates	Measures of impairment	Measures of social support	Measures of depression	
		Disease specific measures			
	Relapses	Pain scales	Measures of disability	Measures of social adjustment	
	Complications	Measures of functional status	Measures of handicap		
		Multidimensional health status profiles and indexes cover many of these dimensions in a single instrument.			

Figure 4.2 Typology of health and associated outcome measures (More information about these different methods is available from the Outcomes Clearing House in Leeds.)

investment and disinvestment chosen?') the Health Service is now starting to use health economics methodologies (see the section on setting priorities, Chapter 5).

The Role of Audit

The aim of medical and clinical audit is to improve patient care by monitoring the whole treatment process – from the moment the patient walks through the door of the surgery to the end of their treatment. This will improve efficiency and standards, by measuring treatment outcomes as well as the input of resources. Health Service audit has developed significantly during the last few years, looking at audits by medical and allied professionals, both in unidisciplinary and multidisciplinary groups.

Further information on the role of audit is given in Chapter 5.

Patient Satisfaction

As mentioned previously, outcomes apply to the whole treatment process, and patients' satisfaction with their treatment is an important part of the audit process. However, there are a number of questions associated with attempting to acquire valid patients' feedback.

First we need to take into account the subjective nature of the patient's views. We need also to have a common definition of what satisfaction is to differentiate between satisfaction, values and expectations. In addition, we need to consider which aspects of healthcare can and should be measured in terms of satisfaction.

Satisfaction could be described as a patient's reaction to the setting, process and result of their experience. Experience is related to a subjective standard, or set of values and expectations. This standard may be one or a combination of the following:

- a subjective ideal or sense of what one deserves;
- a subjective comparison of present and past experiences in similar situations;
- an idea of some minimal acceptable standard.

Working through these considerations makes it easier to assign importance to the positioning and value of patient satisfaction information. This in turn will identify the limitations of this form of evaluation and provide some guidance for additional methods to be used.

The Role of Questionnaires

These can be used when we need to produce data which are more statistically reliable than qualitative methods of measuring patient satisfaction. They can therefore be used to generate a comprehensive view of patient and consumer opinion. Questionnaires can indicate the quality of care provided to patients, particularly when used over a period of time. By using follow-up surveys, changes in the quality of care can be identified, as can any effective changes made as a result of previous surveys. Survey results can be used to set minimum acceptable standards for future plans and allow patients to prioritize from a list of potential new facilities or services. This is tackled in more detail in the priority setting section of Chapter 5.

Chapter 5

Planning for Health Gain

Health gain is the *raison d'être* of the Health Service and this chapter explores it in some depth, looking at aspects of how the Health Service can and should be delivering to a health gain agenda.

The chapter includes the following parts of the health gain process – health needs assessment at both an individual and population level; setting priorities for health service delivery; setting targets for achievement in the field of health gain; compiling action plans (similar methodology to Chapter 2); and methods of monitoring results, including clinical, medical and multidisciplinary audit in more detail than in the previous chapter.

Health Gain

Health gain has been explained as 'adding life to years and years to life'. Adding years to life: this looks at the dimension where there is an increase in life expectancy and reduction in premature death. The goal of adding life to years is to implement plans that will benefit patients by increasing years lived free from ill health, reducing or minimizing the adverse effects of illness and disability, promoting healthy life-styles, physical and social environments and, overall, improving quality of life.

The principles of health gain are completely in tune with the values of the people who will make it work – the healthcare professionals.

The Health Gain Cycle

The key to achieving health gain involves adopting a methodical approach that can be described as the Health Gain Cycle. It also offers an NHS perspective on the planning questions we asked in Chapter 1, as shown in Figure 5.1.

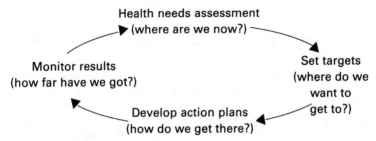

Figure 5.1 The health gain cycle

By depicting these questions in the form of a circle, it can be seen clearly that the knowledge gained in the Monitoring results part of the process then becomes the starting point for the next cycle asking the question 'Where are we now?'. The health status of the local population should have improved as a consequence of the action plans that were implemented to achieve the previously set objectives. The aim is to create a continuous upward spiral of improving health and healthcare by delivering appropriate resources and treatments where they are most needed.

Step 1. Health Needs Assessment (Where Are We Now?)

Before we make any plans we need first to understand the current health status of our population, whether that is local (practice or Health Authority/Health Board size), regional or national. Health needs assessment (HNA) is useful for this purpose. It has been described as 'the process of assessing health status and highlighting areas where changes are needed to improve health and to indicate the nature or direction of those changes'.

Health Authorities are required to:

- review regularly the health of the local population and identify areas for improvement;
- define policy aims and set quantifiable service objectives;
- relate decisions taken about the distribution of resources to their impact on health and objectives identified;
- monitor and evaluate the progress towards their stated policy aims, including the development of outcome indicators.

Ideally such reviews should be done with the participation of local GPs. As their practice computer systems become more sophisticated and they collect more information, the databases can often generate helpful needs assessment information.

The Size of the Problem

But what are the needs of the local population? And how are these different from demands, or even the services available locally? To what extent do those needs coincide with the demands of the population and the services available to meet them? Where there is no overlap priorities need to be decided with the ultimate aim of moving the areas of need, demand and supply so they coincide. Figure 5.2 illustrates how the three areas of need, demand and supply interrelate.

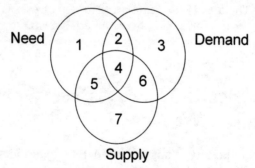

Figure 5.2 Need, demand and supply

Key to Figure 5.2

1. Undeclared and unmet areas of potential benefit (eg middle-aged man unaware of his asthma, hypertension or diabetes).
2. Declared but unmet need (eg waiting list for surgery).

3. Unjustifiable and unmet need (eg tattoo removal, other than for severe emotional or social reasons such as employability).
4. Need and demand is met.
5. Needed services provided without initiation by the patient (eg targeted health promotion for diet or smoking or disease management clinics).
6. Services supplied to meet demand, not need (eg hospitalization for minor surgery which could be managed in general practice).
7. Unused services.

Ideally, the map generated will show a large part of needs, demands and services meeting in area 4 with little investment or provision for area 7.

Information on the size of the problem is usually generated through the public health function in Health Authorities and Health Boards. Need is based on an epidemiological assessment of the incidence and prevalence of disease in a particular population. Epidemiology is a particular public health skill (a specialist competency). An epidemiological approach leads to the assumption that if the cost or burden of illness is large, priority is high; where it is small, priority is low. Once local health needs have been identified their comparison and evaluation with national data enables you to identify key areas. You can use certain criteria to assist in identifying those key areas correctly, for example by asking:

- Is the condition a major cause of premature death or avoidable ill health (sickness and/or disability) either in the population as a whole or among specific groups?
- Are effective interventions possible, offering significant scope for improvement in health?
- Is it possible to set objectives and targets to monitor progress (ie outcome indicators)?

By using available sources of information and applying the above criteria it is possible to pinpoint key areas of local need which, in looking through a number of local public health reports, includes conditions such as asthma. The effectiveness of this activity will depend on:

- making sure the purchasing organization has an effective intelligence gathering function;
- ensuring that local networks are strong and that the relationship between staff involved in purchasing or commissioning and those involved in providing and receiving the services (healthcare professionals and patients) is good;
- putting in place structured approaches to intelligence gathering to provide a common approach. This could involve:
  - disease based health needs assessment (eg using DoH epidemiological research model)
  - population sub-group health needs assessment
  - health needs assessment of geographic areas (eg at electoral ward or locality level).

Practice Based Health Needs Assessment

Having looked at the concepts behind HNA, we now look at how it works in the general practice setting – what sort of information is required, and how to collect, organize and audit the data. From there, the next step is to look at HNA from the point of view of setting priorities – what values, tools and techniques are available, and how we go about shifting resources and changing (where necessary) the ways in which healthcare is provided.

This section focuses on primary care, partly because the process for commissioning secondary care is evolving rapidly with the contracting process, fundholding and the development of a 'primary care led NHS', but also because primary care is the area where the GP has greatest direct control over any changes.

The NHS mission statement (see page 15) shows that the government is focusing the NHS towards delivering a *health* service as opposed to a *disease* service; the aim being to improve health and focus on those who *need* a health service. This has therefore raised the profile of HNA.

Implicit in the mission statement is the assumption that healthcare can go some way towards meeting that need. But, increasingly, people are making that assumption explicit, and so outcomes are defined in terms that are measurable and quantifiable. Admittedly this area is still in its developing phase, but the direction is clear.

From the point of view of supply, the NHS needs to know what services are available; whether they are designed to meet needs, or demands, or both; and how these are assessed and evaluated.

What information is available to general practice?

The NHS is awash with data. Everyone has to collect it – GPs, Health Authorities, Trusts, regional offices and so on. The problem is that data collected unselectively, and often duplicated, can be meaningless. Data has to be turned into information to be useful – and sometimes finding the right data to provide information is difficult. But just because it is hard to find does not mean it should be ignored.

To make the task of collecting data easier, it may be useful to select key areas. These are some examples of criteria for selection:

- major areas of high morbidity, mortality or disability (physical and psychological);
- areas that occupy large amounts of time and resource in the NHS;
- areas where choices exist between different management options or between different providers of similar services;
- national and regional priorities (eg Health of the Nation);
- local GP and community concerns;
- areas where there are a significant number of life years lost;
- areas where quality of life can be substantially improved;
- areas where it is possible to set objectives and targets to monitor progress.

These are some examples of where you might find useful data:

- government statistics (eg Office of Population Census and Surveys);
- epidemiology studies (national or local, usually run by public health);
- surveys – of patients (qualitative); of the public (eg Gallup);
- charities, voluntary groups, patient support groups;
- university- and medical school-sponsored research;
- clinical studies;
- local medical audit (practice data).

Making effective use of the data is not always easy. Data collected from different sources by different people with different priorities may end up meaningless. It is important to collect data in a structured and planned way. Who is collecting what? How will the data be collected and organized? Making sure everyone works together through good networks and good relationships is key to successful information gathering.

So, in summary, the first step is to select key areas, maybe only a few at a time, so that the task remains manageable. This is sometimes referred to as working with 'bite-sized chunks' and is certainly useful advice. Collect the data and then analyse the information to identify the needs of the local population. Having assessed the needs – and by that I mean not only areas of need but also amount of need – it is also important to assess how that need is currently being met. For example, some years ago, one of the Regional Health Authorities looked at visual impairment in the elderly as a possible area of health need. The data showed this was clearly an area of 'unmet need', as illustrated in Table 5.1.

Table 5.1 Visual impairment in the elderly

Total population
14–16% reported sight problems

Over 75s
23–25% reported sight problems. Of these:

- 40% reported sudden deterioration in last six months
- 25% had not had a sight test in the last two years
- 50% were unregistered, had not heard of registration
- 60% had at least five coexisting health problems compared to 29% in the sighted group

In a second example, looking at different management approaches to stroke patients, a number of questions should be raised. Stroke affects two people in every 1,000 each year. It currently uses 4 per cent of the total NHS budget. Patients with stroke occupy 12 per cent of medical speciality beds in hospitals.

Most survivors recover rapidly in the first three months, regardless of whether they receive formal rehabilitation. A study in the early 1990s found no difference between the improvement of a group receiving speech therapy as opposed to no speech therapy. There is also evidence that community rehabilitation is effective. There is no *significant* difference between supported volunteers and professionals.

The difficulty with such implicit comparisons is that the two cases are completely different. It may be extremely difficult, if not impossible, to deprive resources from one area, say stroke patients, to allocate to a totally separate area, say visual impairment. A review of six different Health Authorities found that it was impossible to agree when comparing different services. The Authorities made more progress by analysing priorities within individual service areas.

Obviously the merging of authorities now makes it much easier, and more relevant, to look at priorities within service or disease areas. Instead of looking at the component costs in isolation the total investment in managing one disease area can be calculated. When taken together with outcome indicators that look at the management option that is best for patients the cost-effectiveness of the treatment can be looked at objectively.

There are now a number of examples where this 'disease management' approach has been looked at, with the result that the pattern of care for patients with a particular disease has been altered.

Nevertheless the issue remains; how do we best assess and meet the health needs of the population, given that the resources available are determined largely by political forces – which is not always something that can be challenged easily.

HNA in general practice – diabetes
This approach was described by a consultant in public health as one worth considering for the management of diabetes in general practice.

- Prevalence of condition, ie
  - number of patients on the practice list;
  - number of patients diagnosed/treated;
  - number of patient consultations each year;
- Treatment options:
  - prevention;
  - treatment, eg diet, insulin, medicines, etc;
  - prevent complications, eg annual checks, patient registers;
  - early treatment of complications, such as blindness;

- patient education, eg self-management;
- Delivery of care – where?
  - primary care;
  - community;
  - hospital.

Of course if the secondary sector was also being considered, hospital referrals, admissions and so on would also need to be taken into account.

A Composite Practice Based Model for HNA

This second example came from a study in Edinburgh that looked at four complementary methods for HNA and came out with a recommendation involving all of them. As a general rule, the following suggestions can be applied anywhere for practices looking to undertake HNA.

1. Start with practice held knowledge and experience of working in the community.
2. Use a public health physician as part of the team to draw up a profile including mortality, morbidity and demographic data.
3. Conduct a rapid participatory appraisal to identify broad areas of perceived health need.
4. Conduct a survey to clarify specific issues as necessary.
5. Help implement and review changes.

Individually, all methods took considerable time and effort, but each yielded different and valuable insights. Furthermore, many health needs stemmed from social and environmental causes and could not be met by health services alone. Collaboration within the local community was very important in this case.

What is currently happening

Some useful general information about GP practice can be obtained from published sources. Government surveys can also provide useful information, which practices can use for comparison. It can be useful to use comparisons with national average data, to determine areas where attention may be needed.

Table 5.2 shows the sort of data that can be found, either by practices themselves, or by asking an information resource to do the search for you.

Table 5.2 Data collection

Causes of death	Annual deaths per 10,000 patients
Heart disease	50
Cancer	25
Stroke	15
Respiratory	15
Others	10
Total	115

Eg 0.5% die of heart disease; 1% of the practice's population dies each year.

Spectrum of morbidity	Conditions
Generalized minor conditions 53% of consultations	The top conditions in this category, by consulting rates, include upper respiratory tract infections, skin disorders, minor trauma, psychiatric and gastrointestinal
Chronic conditions 32% of consultations	The key areas here are: cardiovascular (high blood pressure, chronic ischaemic heart disease, heart failure), respiratory (asthma, chronic bronchitis), gastrointestinal, diabetes and the after-effects of stroke
Severe/major conditions 15% of consultations	This area includes acute bronchitis, pneumonia, severe depression, acute myocardial infarction, all new cancers, acute stroke, acute abdominal disorders

One way of doing HNA is to look at it as a proportion of NHS spend, and Table 5.3 shows where the bulk of NHS expenditure takes place.

Another way of looking at the provision of existing services is to see what activities the NHS is most concerned with.

In 1992/93 in England, the total number of operations was 5,068,594. The top ten procedures in this list account for 23.3 per cent of all operations. These include: upper GI endoscopy (300,000), terminations (150,000), cystoscopy (150,000), Ds and Cs (125,000), teeth extractions (90,000), cataract surgery (90,000), tonsillectomies (75,000), corrections of 'glue ear' (70,000), hernia

Table 5.3 NHS Expenditure (Source: Warner et al, 1995)

Ten main causes	As % of NHS spend 1989–90
1. Injury and poisoning	5.4%
2. Schizophrenia	5.4%
3. Mouth disease	4.8%
4. Mental retardation	4.4%
5. Symptoms	4.0%
6. Stroke	4.0%
7. Normal pregnancy and delivery	3.9%
8. Ischaemic heart disease	3.6%
9. Ulcers and stomach	2.8%
10. Skin infections	2.6%

repairs (60,000), and hysterectomies (60,000). It is interesting to note that two out of the top three are diagnostic. There is also some information to suggest that some of these procedures do not contribute to health gain in every case. These are areas which are being investigated by the Centre for Reviews and Dissemination at York.

In terms of HNA there is another measure of health outcomes – that of years of potential life lost before age 85. OPCS published data in 1986 for England and Wales in 1984 which indicated the top ten causes, some of which later became Health of the Nation target areas.

Asthma Case Study

This case study has been used a number of times with Health Authorities and GP fundholders. When introduced at a pilot workshop on priority setting, delegates said they found it extremely useful to see the picture from the Health Authority or purchaser viewpoint.

The data compare local with national data and, as we discussed earlier, the variances act as a useful focus for areas that may require further attention and analyses. Variances may or may not be significant according to local factors, but they are a good starting point.

The figures in Table 5.4 relate activity, eg patient visits and costs.

Table 5.4 Asthma – activity and cost

	Variance against national average	
GP consultation	–2%	–£3K
GP chronic disease clinics	–34%	?
GP prescribing cost	–9%	–£50K
GP referrals	+22%	+£6K
Hospital admissions	+9%	+£35K

Table 5.5 Asthma – health needs and outcome

	Expenditure	Actual	Various
Prevalence	?	?	0
Mortality	11	16	+5
Poor quality of life	19%	27%	+42%
Readmission rates	?10	30%	
	(Upper Park)	(Grand Union)	

The figures in Table 5.5 look at the outcome indicators, eg mortality and morbidity, quality of life, and treatment in the primary and secondary sectors.

Clinical Issues

We asked Health Authorities to consider the case study from a number of perspectives – clinical, provider and purchaser. These are some of the clinical pointers for discussion.

- How good is patient self-management? Are they able to use peak flow meters?
- Are patients being managed according to any best practice guidelines (or, indeed, any guidelines at all)?
- What shared care arrangements are in place to manage the patient across the primary/secondary care interface? Do the IT links exist/support this?
- What clinical audit and training is in place?
- What quality measures are there to judge the providers?

Provider Issues

In terms of delivering care to manage asthma disease in the local population, how are these services best provided? And by whom? There are a number of alternatives.

- What about a strengthened primary care team?
- What about a community asthma nurse or a community based clinic?
- What is the role of community Trust staff, practice staff and the acute Trust?
- Who is best placed to deal with the preventative side of management?
- Should the hospitals have an open door policy for outpatients?
- What specialization, if any, do consultants have to deal with asthmatics?

Purchasing Issues

As purchasers responsible for 'purchasing' the total services, what type of issues might arise?

- How best to purchase for an appropriate mix of services, fostering the shift from hospital to the community and primary care teams where possible?
- Who purchases what? What consistency is there between purchasing by the Health Authority or Health Board and fundholders?
- What shall the contracts specify for quality measures?

- How shall purchasers monitor?
- What targets should be set?

In the end it is important to take all the issues as a whole to help provide appropriate services; appropriate for the primary and secondary sectors; and appropriate, given the financial constraints of the real world and the difficulties in dealing with the public's voice - eg the Patients' Charter.

In considering the difficult choices that purchasers have to make it is useful to get clinical input. A useful question to ask at this point is what elements, factors or events would be *unacceptable* for the management of the disease – those factors may include personal ones such as night calls which disrupt a clinician's sleep – and the patient's! The question to ask is therefore 'What would you *not* like to happen?'

Lessons From Practice Based HNA

- It takes time – more than originally thought, in most cases.
- Data cannot be analysed easily from existing GP computer systems – sometimes a manual trawl through records is best – if time consuming (see above).
- Many people are involved in the HNA process – not just practice staff.
- Information is incomplete – and usually in the wrong place.
- Sharing information, issues and debate are of great value.

On occasion, the choices made result in having to make changes to the way certain services are provided. This will be considered later in the chapter.

Step 2. Setting Targets

'Cheshire Puss,' she began rather timidly, 'Would you tell me please, which way I ought to go from here?'
'That depends a good deal on where you want to go,' said the Cat.
'I don't much care where,' said Alice.
'Then it doesn't much matter which way you go,' said the Cat.

Lewis Carroll, *Alice's Adventures in Wonderland.*

The message is clear. To achieve health gain it is necessary to have a clear idea of where you are now (health needs assessment), where you want to be in the future (target setting) and how to get there (action plans).

Table 5.6 Key areas for health gain

	England	Wales	Scotland	Northern Ireland
Coronary heart disease and stroke	✓	✓	✓	✓
Cancers	✓	✓	✓	✓
Accidents/injuries	✓	✓	✓	✓
Mental illness	✓	✓		✓
HIV/AIDS and sexual health	✓		✓	
Maternal and child health		✓		✓
Mental handicap		✓		
Respiratory disease		✓		✓
Physical disability and discomfort		✓		✓
Healthy environments		✓		
Emotional health and relationships		✓		
Dental and oral health			✓	
Child care				✓
Misuse of drugs			✓	
Smoking			✓	
Drinking		✓		

Health Authorities and Health Boards are likely to base their health strategies, at least in part, on any strategies emanating from the national offices. In England, this means the Health of the Nation. The five key areas for health gain for the UK as a whole are shown in Table 5.6. In each key area for England targets have been set which are timebound to be achieved by 2002. The critical success factors associated with the Health of the Nation targets are:

- a focus on measurable improvements in health (health gain);
- being people-centred – valuing people as individuals and managing services to that end;
- resource-effectiveness – striving to achieve the most cost-effective balance in the use of available resources.

Quality Markers

A range of indicators can be applied to targets in each key area to show the change in health status, both for the population as a whole and for individuals.

- **Mortality** eg reduction in mortality or reduction in avoidable deaths; increase in life expectancy.
- **Morbidity** eg reduction in incidence; reduction in prevalence; reduction in preventable ill health; minimize the effects of disease; maximize symptom control; absence of disease; reversal or stabilization of disease.
- **Physical function** eg ability to feed; improved ambulation; ability to dress; ability to bathe.
- **Psychological function** eg reduction in anxiety; acceptance of death (terminal care).
- **Unplanned use of care** eg reduction in readmissions; reduction in complication rates; reduction in number of prolonged stays; reduction in prolonged courses of treatment.
- **Occupational functions** eg decrease in days off work/school.
- **Health-related knowledge and behaviour** eg increased understanding by patient of their condition; increased compliance with treatment; more lifestyle advice given; changed behaviour patterns (reduced alcohol/tobacco consumption, increased exercise, diet changes);
- **Patient satisfaction** eg increased access to services; increased convenience; increased perception of quality; increased equality.

To decide which policy options are appropriate to reduce morbidity and mortality in disease areas it is helpful to identify the causative factors.

Questions at this point to assist in setting targets include the following.

Morbidity

- What reduction in symptoms can be achieved?
- Can normal activity be resumed?
- What reduction can be made in hospital admissions?

Mortality

- Is local mortality higher than national mortality for this condition?
- What local targets for reduction in mortality exist?

Management

- How many effective disease management clinics/clinical guidelines are in operation?
- How often are patients/clinical guidelines reviewed?

Given the above list of quality markers, it should be possible to generate more disease-specific objectives that fall out of the needs assessment exercise. In this way a set of meaningful indicators can be used to judge the success of the organization.

Here is an example of how these measures can be applied to different disease areas, in this case, asthma. Target setting for asthma management suggests that:

1. The goal of asthma management is that patients should be symptom free.
2. There is evidence that morbidity and mortality from asthma is not improving in the UK, despite an increase in the amount of treatment prescribed. This suggests that current management is not achieving 'best practice' as defined from evidence and opinion leaders.
3. Targets in asthma management could, for example, focus on detection and early and effective treatment of the disease. Another fruitful area for target setting is education; providing information to both patients and carers in the optimal management of the illness, and instruction on how to recognize signs of serious disease in order to take prompt action.

Examples of targets may include:

Morbidity/Mortality

- to reduce morbidity rate;
- to reduce mortality rate;
- reduction in patients having daily symptoms;
- reduction in patients waking at night with asthma;
- reduction in patients with activity restriction;
- reduction in need for relief medication (eg short acting inhaled bronchodilation) to less than two or three times a week;
- increase proportion of patients with no time lost from work or school;
- reduction in hospital admissions for acute attacks;
- improvement in quality of life scores on appropriate quality of life scale.

Management

- every GP to have a systematic approach to the diagnosis of asthma;
- all asthmatics to be invited for regular review at least once a year;
- practices to be running asthma clinics according to guidelines developed from best practice evidence, in consultation with colleagues;
- practices to hold register of all asthmatics;
- practices to audit asthma care according to guidelines developed from best practice evidence, in consultation with colleagues;
- asthma training available to all practice nurses running asthma clinics;
- set up system for recording and monitoring hospital admissions;
- asthmatics have a guided self-management plan, where appropriate;
- asthmatics to be provided with a peak flow meter and taught how to use it;
- all patients with asthma to have respiratory physiology testing;
- management plans developed with colleagues across primary and secondary care (eg admission, referral and discharge criteria, GP follow-up after acute admission, patient education on discharge).

Education

- patients on inhaled medication to receive training in inhaled technique;
- patients to be educated to recognize signs of deterioration of asthma and to know appropriate action to take;
- patients on prophylactic (preventive) medication to be educated about the rationale for taking regular medication regardless of symptom frequency;
- asthma training a prerequisite for all practice nurses running asthma clinics;
- availability of information/training for school teachers about asthma and its treatment.

Setting priorities

Since 1990 a great deal of interest has been generated, largely as a result of the NHS reforms, in planning healthcare according to priorities. The purchaser/provider split has raised the importance of effective, reasonable and acceptable resource allocation.

It is generally recognized that resources for healthcare have always been, and will always be, finite. This is not simply a problem for the UK, but universally applicable for both developed and developing countries. In view of this, there are three 'must do's to ensure healthcare resources for a given population are used to best effect:

1. Improvements in the efficiency of healthcare management
2. Targeting services at those parts of the population in need
3. Employing those interventions which are effective or cost-effective

Taking decisions on priorities based on the way services were provided historically has possibly led to a level of unmet need in the population for which there were technological solutions available. As a consequence, the NHS reforms are encouraging Health Authorities and Boards to make more explicit choices about what services they can afford to purchase for their populations. In doing so, Authorities are faced with the need to consider carefully how resources are allocated to different client groups, conditions and treatments.

A number of dilemmas have been highlighted in this process of making choices. These dilemmas are expressed as the choice between:

- prevention rather than intervention;
- saving life rather than improving quality of life;
- primary and community health services rather than secondary or tertiary hospital care;
- individual need rather than population requirements;
- well-known articulated demands rather than less popular health need;
- high volume, low cost versus low volume, high cost.

In addition there is a view that purchasing shifts are required if national and local health gain objectives are to be achieved. Movement from secondary to primary care is encouraged and developing community based care for people is seen as a priority. This has resulted in an active research programme and practical work in planning priorities, making choices and using resources effectively.

Subjectivity and variability are barriers to objective decision making in any situation. However, given the often conflicting pressures acting on the health manager, it can be difficult for us to adopt a logical approach to setting priorities. In looking at HNA, it becomes obvious that resources have to be allocated and spread between many therapy or disease areas. But on what criteria? And what are the issues behind these choices? Are there any methodologies that can help? Priorities must be to:

- cure, relieve and comfort (disease);
- promote (health) and prevent (disease and disability);
- rehabilitate (to health and fitness).

These are, however, generalized priorities. As an added complication, healthcare in today's political climate is also having to face the issue of 'selecting priorities' – nobody likes to use terms such as rationing but that effectively is what it is.

The role of the purchaser is to secure improvements in the health of the population by ensuring that services are made available in response to identified health needs and with regard to the wishes of individuals. With the purchaser/provider split within the NHS, the purchaser's role has been further defined. Most GPs carry that 'purchaser' responsibility in one form or another. 'Health needs' and 'wishes of individuals' must be recognized – but how?

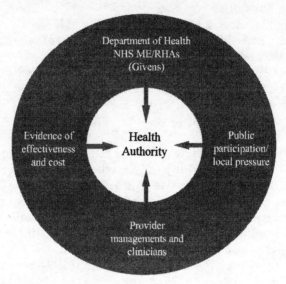

Figure 5.3 'Doughnut' diagram (Reproduced with kind permission of Professor Chris Ham, HSMC, 1994)

Based on work done with Southampton and South West Hampshire Health Authority, this 'doughnut' diagram was devised to examine the pressures on those responsible for allocating resources.

The vertical axis reflects the traditional pressures – those of the government – the national dictats or givens. These include targets on reduction in waiting times, screening programmes, Health of the Nation areas, etc. From the bottom are those pressures of the local providers who traditionally have demanded funds and investment for their hospital services without necessarily any supporting evidence or justification of their need. This has sometimes been called planning by decibels.

The horizontal axis introduces the more recent, and also politically driven, pressures. This includes public participation, eg Patients' Charter or formally through the Community Health

Council or public surveys and meetings. On the other side is the pressure from evidence – ie evidence of needs, effectiveness and costs, which is transformed into decisions on rational evidence-based treatment, or a cost-effective decision making process.

There are of course many other pressures. In addition to government targets or givens there are also more local targets, eg Authority targets, targets at practice level, patient targets and also possibly personal targets.

But, whatever the pressures, there will always remain the dilemma of insufficient resources to satisfy all of the demands for which some kind of medical, surgical or rehabilitative intervention is feasible. Then the aim has to be to maximize productivity of available resources by investing in the most cost-effective treatment options – indeed to deliver the greatest health gain for the money spent.

In order to set useful priorities, therefore, information has to be collected from all interested parties. The role of purchaser involves fair arbitration between the competing interests and infusing the decision making with available evidence.

Assessing needs – burdens of disease analysis
Traditionally, one of the common approaches has been to examine the burdens of any disease. Burden analysis involves both epidemiologists and economists working together looking at the numbers of sufferers and the costs involved. The types of information needed are as follows, using asthma as an example.

Prevalence – the number of sufferers. Around 10 per cent of children experience wheezing in a 12-month period. For adults, between 2 per cent and 5 per cent are diagnosed asthmatic. This amounts to about 2 million asthma sufferers in the UK.

Direct costs – those resources used to prevent, detect and treat the disease (costs borne essentially by the NHS). The estimated costs to the NHS for asthma management in 1990 for GP consultations, medicines, in-patient and out-patient treatment in hospital were £405 million. When adjusted to 1992 prices this rose to £472.4 million.

Indirect costs – loss of productive output caused by sickness, absence, etc (costs to the wider community). In 1991/92 the following calculations were made for the indirect costs associated with asthma. Eleven million days lost from work; 1.9 per cent of all certified days lost from work; sickness and invalidity benefits cost DSS £101 million; all indicating lost potential productivity of £558.33 million (by using average earnings). These are costs incurred as a result of not being able to do something else – and for which payment is due. They are sometimes referred to as the costs to the community.

Personal costs – disability, pain, psychological distress, etc (costs to the patient). These costs are much more subjective. They relate to the patient as an individual, and it is therefore much more difficult to generalize as the severity of disease varies widely between patients – and over time. However, studies have shown that 50 per cent of asthma patients experience at least one attack requiring medical attention over 12 months. Of these, 47 per cent have one attack; 22 per cent have two attacks; 31 per cent have three or more.

Additionally, 73 per cent of patients wake one night per week and 39 per cent wake each night. For children, the picture is as uncomfortable: 58 per cent have reported wheezing and experience school absence as a consequence. Of these, 12 per cent lose 30 days or more in a year.

A more sophisticated approach to needs assessment involves equating need with ability to benefit. The priority then rests not only on the size of the problem but on the evidence of ability to benefit. One definition of this ability is to consider the years of potential life lost before the average life expectancy is reached (taken as either 75 or 85 depending on who is compiling the information). A third level of sophistication is equating need and ability to benefit with the availability of effective interventions. There are often alternative interventions available that could usefully be compared, both on clinical and economic evidence.

Use of burden data measures the amount of ill health caused by different diseases. It can be used to indicate relative needs to help prioritize the allocation of resources. Use of burden data provides more than mortality and morbidity data. These measures can also provide baseline data against which the impact of an intervention may be assessed, can assist in healthcare planning and can help determine medical research priorities. There are limitations with the application of burden data. First, with the measures of direct costs, estimates are based on treatment and care supplied – but are these appropriate levels? Second, when looking at the indirect costs (which are largely productivity losses), how is sickness absence from work valued? And are retired individuals less 'valued'? Third, burden measures encourage the view that if an illness is costly more resources should be committed to its treatment. However, this does not take into account the effectiveness of the treatment used.

The economic approach

A different way of looking at resource management is through the economic approach. Economists would argue that resources should be deployed to have maximum impact in improving health. By using this method resources will be allocated to those treatments that contribute most to reducing health need per healthcare pound spent. The focus is therefore on the treatments and not on the disease areas, as it is when looking at burdens of disease analysis.

The availability and costs of interventions

Given the technological advances since the inception of the Health Service in diagnosing and treating diseases, it is not surprising that there are a range of available options for using scarce resources in any given situation. Deciding to use resources in one way inevitably means giving up the chance to use them in other desirable ways. The benefits given up in the best alternative use of resources are called the 'opportunity cost'.

CASE STUDY

This case study is adapted from a paper by Eddy (1992) and illustrates the different approaches with a numerical example.

For the purposes of the case study, Units of health benefit (UHBs) = Quality adjusted life years (QALYs) or Healthy year equivalents. These are important as a means of comparing totally different therapy areas.

So, to illustrate the principle, treatment A has been assessed as generating 9.5 units of health benefit when given to an individual. The cost per procedure is £3,000. In our population there

Table 5.7 Example of purchasing treatments

Treatment	Units of health benefit	Cost	Patients	Total UHBs	Total cost	C/E ratio
A	9.5	£3,000	20	190	£60,000	£316
B	9.0	£3,800	15	135	£57,000	£422
C	8.6	£2,300	30	258	£69,000	£267
D	8.3	£1,000	5	42	£5,000	£119
E	7.5	£5,200	70	525	£364,000	£693
F	6.8	£950	40	272	£38,000	£140
G	5.4	£3,000	84	454	£252,000	£555
H	4.3	£2,200	18	77	£39,600	£512
I	4.0	£875	65	260	£56,875	£219
J	3.8	£300	50	190	£15,000	£80
			397	2,403	£956,475	

are 20 patients who could benefit from the treatment, giving a total benefit of 190 UHBs. The cost for treating all 20 patients is £60,000 (20 times £3,000). The cost-effectiveness ratio is therefore 316. The other treatments have been rated in the same way.

By providing treatments to all available patients, the service would treat 397 patients at a total cost of £956,475 and generate a total of 2,403 UHBs. However, in the real world, choices have to be made. The Authority has only £600,000 instead of £956,475. There is therefore a dilemma in deciding which treatment(s) to purchase.

There are a number of different perspectives.

Option 1: the medical approach – in which the most effective treatment is chosen, followed by the next most effective and so on, until the money runs out. As treatment A is most effective, followed by B, this approach would allow treatment of all patients needing treatments A to F inclusive – a total of 180 patients. This would cost the Authority £588,000 and generate a total of 1,422 UHBs.

Option 2: the epidemiologist's approach – benefiting the greatest number. In this option only treatments E and G would be funded, with 154 patients benefiting at a cost of £616,000 and generating only 979 UHBs. However, the Authority is overspent with this option and has achieved less health gain using the UHB measure.

Option 3: the economic approach – which chooses the most cost-effective treatments until the budget is exhausted. With this option all treatments except E are funded. The total cost is £592,475 – within budget, the number of patients treated is 327 and the total number of UHBs generated is 1,878.

The conclusion from this case study is that, for any resource limit, ordering treatments by their cost-effectiveness ratios will deliver more benefit than any other method of ranking.

There have been attempts in real life to use this theoretical approach; for example, QALYs. Table 5.8 (reproduced from work by Alan Maynard and colleagues from the University of York) gives a list of treatments that have been analysed by economists and published in the literature. The cost per QALY has been calculated and is ranked accordingly.

Table 5.8 Cost per QALY for various interventions (Source: Drummond and Maynard, 1993)

Treatment	Cost per QALY (August 1990) (£)
Cholesterol testing and treatment by diet (adults aged 40–69)	220
Neurosurgical intervention for head injury	240
Advice to stop smoking from general practitioner	270
Neurosurgical intervention for subarachnoid haemorrhage	490
Antihypertensive treatment to prevent stroke (aged 45–64)	940
Pacemaker implantation	1,100
Hip replacement	1,180
Valve replacement for aortic stenosis	1,140
Cholesterol testing and treatment	1,480
Coronary artery bypass graft (patients with left main vessel disease, severe angina)	2,090
Kidney transplantation	4,710
Breast cancer screening	5,780
Heart transplantation	7,840
Cholesterol testing and treatment (incrementally) of all adults aged 25–39	14,150
Home haemodialysis	17,260

Coronary artery bypass graft (patients with one vessel disease, moderate angina)	18,830
Continuous ambulatory peritoneal dialysis	19,870
Hospital haemodialysis	21,970
Erythropoietin for anaemia in patients receiving dialysis (assuming 10% reduction in mortality)	54,380
Neurosurgical intervention for malignant intracranial tumours	107,780
Erythropoietin for anaemia in patients receiving dialysis (assuming no increase in survival)	126,290

However, the case study does raise some issues.

The economic approach looks at cost-effectiveness, and this means examining both costs *and* outcomes in detail. We already recognize there are certain limitations with cost data and we try to make assessments for these. But what about outcomes? Are the measures robust? Are they relevant and can they be applied with validity across different disease areas, treatments, people, or even over time? QALYs attempt this, but there are concerns.

1. About the accuracy of the data. Who makes the judgements upon which the decisions are taken and which methods have been used in collecting the data in the first place?
2. QALYs discriminate against the elderly.
3. Who is to say that the value of a year of life is constant throughout that life?
4. There are a number of ethical considerations and, in addition, QALYs ignore the carers, where there are also economic and quality of life considerations.
5. Economics takes the population view, which can sometime conflict with the doctor's concern with the individual patient. Where a doctor is concerned with the individual patient the prevalence of a disease does not currently affect the priority of its treatment.

Given all the complexities and confusions it is important to consider how best to use this for the future – the experts mostly advise the incremental step-by-step approach.

So, to conclude, the way forward in using heath economic information is to use it to focus on costs and benefits of changing care provision in specific areas. Programmes should be selected for study where there is some consistency of outputs between them and where cost can be measured. A mix of services within programmes can be examined to see whether a change in spend (by reallocating it) will result in more benefits. To assist this process, it is helpful to:

- decide which treatments are so valuable that it would be a waste of time to analyse them;
- of the rest, decide which areas are most open to change;
- identify the costs and benefits of the options;
- measure and value the costs and benefits by use of research and the existing literature;
- move to progressively more difficult areas.

However, there are a few points to watch. A pure economic approach is unworkable in the real world, when used in isolation. It is an important, but not sole, contributor to the process of purchasing.

Choices in Healthcare

As part of an exercise in setting priorities some work has been done in identifying the values that guide the thinking of the purchasing organization. In summary, organizations recognize the different drivers that operate in taking decisions and are able to formulate a set of values that characterizes the way in which decisions are made. It is important to be able to justify these in a public setting, when the process of decision making is as transparent as the end result.

For example, in one group that conducted this exercise, the different values identified by the group were effectiveness, efficiency, numbers of people involved – impact, equity and prevention.

Other groups who have undertaken the exercise have suggested the following criteria as values behind decision making:

- greatest good for the greatest number;
- prevalence of the problem and the consequences of not treating;

- access and availability of appropriate services;
- quality of life;
- emotion and personal knowledge or expertise;
- cost or cost-effectiveness.

Having established a core set of values, it is useful to revisit this list after a case study in priority setting has been undertaken to see how closely actual decision making mirrors the aspirational intentions of the organization. For example, a group attempting this exercise may identify cost and personal knowledge as their two main considerations over a consideration of cost-effectiveness or the quality of life for patients.

As we have seen, purchasing decisions are guided by a number of influencing factors some of which we have discussed, along with the increasing importance of evidence-based decision making. A 1995 survey among decision makers in Scotland identified the factors involved from their perspective together with a weighting assigned to each (two for high influence and one for some influence). The results are shown in Table 5.9.

Table 5.9 Weightings given to factors in decision making (*Health Service Journal*, 1995)

Factor	Weighting
Public health doctors	70
Local priorities	70
Finance resources	69
Scottish Office priorities	68
Opinion of GPs	65
Statistical data	64
Knowledge about local providers	63
Clinicians' opinions	59
Own professional experience	53
National politics	49
Local politics	49
Opinion of local advisory bodies	47
Evidence from the literature	46
Consumer opinion	46
Own intuition/hunch	39
Health economics	35

The survey indicated how embryonic the availability of evidence and health economics information is. It is likely, as more information is collated and disseminated, that the weightings attached to these factors will increase.

Resource Shifting

When we make decisions about resource use and about priority setting in healthcare we usually consider changes to existing levels of service provision and not just whether an entire service should or should not be provided. Any decision about which changes are pursued should be informed with respect to costs and benefits of change from the established baselines (what we are doing now). So the sensible approach is to look at changes at the margin, in terms of costs and benefits – marginal analysis. In this context 'marginal' refers to 'at the margin' not 'unimportant'.

The government has quite clearly laid out that the NHS will judge its results under three headings: Equity, Efficiency, Responsiveness. Equity involves targeting resources where the needs are greatest; efficiency considers both clinical effectiveness and value for money; responsiveness addresses meeting the needs of individual patients and responding, as needs change and as medical knowledge advances. Considering these together, rather than in isolation, uncovers inherent conflicts that pose dilemmas for the NHS. It is possible that, in addressing the requirements of one of these criteria, we will make addressing others impossible.

Added to this, with the development and drive towards a primary care led NHS, there are no doubt increasing pressures on the need to examine the way resources are allocated and the need, perhaps, to shift more healthcare into the primary sector. This, however, is difficult to achieve, when most resources are tied up in secondary care facilities and services.

The government is now explicitly stating certain values that underpin and add to the pressures outlined earlier. If resources are to be invested – and in some cases even disinvested – what are the criteria for doing so? How can this be achieved in a practical way? What have other Authorities done?

Efficiency must be a preoccupation of any organization when planning. In the NHS this revolves around considerations of 'clinical effectiveness' and 'value for money'. How can these be found?

Doing the most effective things, measured in good outcomes for patients, must be the central interest of both commissioners and providers. It is estimated that 85 per cent of interventions have never been scientifically proven to be effective, which should call into question where resources are allocated.

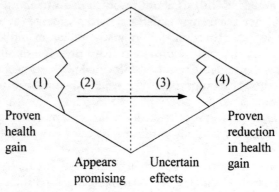

Figure 5.4 The health gain rhomboid

The rhomboid shown in Figure 5.4 was developed by the Welsh Health Planning Forum, following work by David Eddy in the US, to illustrate the view that, of all healthcare interventions, there is only evidence of effectiveness for about 15 per cent of procedures. Conversely, around 15 per cent of interventions currently used may actually be harmful. This means that up to 70 per cent of what is currently done may be promising, or possibly useful, but we can't be sure without the 'gold standard' support of a randomized clinical trial; or that 70 per cent may not be effective, and more evaluation is required because the evidence for effectiveness is not there yet. Other commentators, eg Sackett, wrote in the *Lancet* (1995) that at least for medical interventions around 70 per cent of decisions were evidence based. So perhaps the situation is improving.

The search for answers to these questions has led to the new discipline of evidence-based decision making – which is led by Sackett's centre in Oxford. In the UK a number of initiatives have been set up to collate and disseminate available evidence, and many of these are now linked internationally to other centres world-wide. They include The Cochrane Centre (Oxford),

Outcomes Clearing House (Leeds), Centre for Reviews and Dissemination (York), Aggressive Research Information Facility (ARIF, West Midlands). In addition there are many local and regional initiatives, whose aim is to produce practical guidance for managers and clinicians. Some booklets have already been published and circulated both at national and at more local level, eg Bandolier from Oxford and East Anglia Region.

The Central Health Outcomes Unit at the Department of Health has developed a model to assist in considering attainment of optimum health outcomes. It represents an approach from the clinical perspective, to identify the value of certain interventions on the various states of health. It works well for management of chronic diseases, and indeed is not too dissimilar from the HNA example for diabetes illustrated earlier.

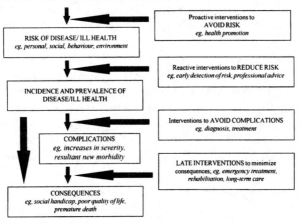

Source: DoH, 1990

Figure 5.5 Population health outcome model

Where there is no evidence based on the results of randomized clinical trials we have to turn to other information sources and different mechanisms to generate results. Alternatives are medical and clinical audit (considered later in this chapter) and the softer areas of patient satisfaction surveys, evaluation of customer complaints and observations over a long period of time. Outcomes for patients can be identified as prevention of 'systems failures' or in terms of improved morbidity, mortality or social functioning, as in the list of quality indicators on page 67.

Many interventions will also involve shifts between sectors of care. For example, switches from secondary to primary care occur:

- if we prevent hospital admissions by, eg out-patients or day case surgery;
- if we encourage early discharge from hospital;
- if we reduce hospital attendance with more 'follow-ups' in general practice.

The use of clinical guidelines and other management plans for diseases will increasingly formalize both best practice and new patterns of service provision, which address both the wishes of patients and the changing role of clinicians and their teams. In theory, this should also change the centres of cost. The critical point is whether resources follow the location of treatment or, rather, how can that be ensured?

There are a number of practical tools to assist in this activity. The first one we look at is the cost mapping exercise, which can be used to identify the resources allocated to diagnosis and management of particular diseases. Once the costs of the current method of treatment have been identified it is easier to determine the impact of a change in approach. One practical application of this is programme budgeting, which has been used locally in the UK.

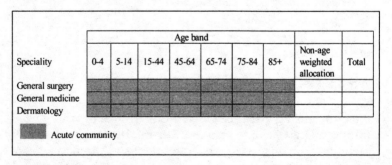

Speciality	Age band							Non-age weighted allocation	Total
	0-4	5-14	15-44	45-64	65-74	75-84	85+		
General surgery									
General medicine									
Dermatology									

Acute/ community

Figure 5.6 Programme budgeting

In this technique budgeted spends are broken down by age bands, speciality, acute and community. By describing them in the grid shown in Figure 5.6 it can be seen which sectors of the community receive most resources and which treatments are currently most costly. A decision can then be taken as to whether the mix and spread is appropriate, or whether some changes are needed. By including information from GP fundholders an accurate picture can be built up of where investments and disinvestments need to occur.

It is possible to identify efficiencies in the process for treating patients. Two types of efficiencies are relevant in this context – operational efficiency, in which a given objective is achieved at least cost; and allocative efficiency, where resources should be allocated to do as much good as possible.

Another technique is that of marginal analysis, mentioned earlier. One Health Authority used this to achieve health gains in maternal and early child health while remaining – and this was key – resource neutral. The working group of 18, representing different interests, were asked to identify ten areas for investment.

1. Health education for children.*
2. Foetal assessment unit.*
3. Support for emotional ill health during and after pregnancy.*
4. Promotion of breast feeding.*
5. Child abuse intervention service.*
6. Targeted family planning.
7. Identification, targeting and support of women with high risk pregnancies.
8. Continuity of care.
9. Counselling (termination, stillbirth, genetic, etc).
10. Community and primary care for children.

The five asterisked were dropped after consultation between the core evaluation team and a joint planning group of Health Authorities.

The group was also asked to identify ten areas for disinvestment.

1. Clinics for childhood surveillance.*
2. Less duplication for family planning services by Health Authority and in general practice.*
3. Increased interval between cervical screens.*
4. Subfertility services.*

5. Parent craft classes, etc.*
6. Admissions to units other than district general hospitals for delivery.*
7. Antenatal care for women with low risk pregnancies.
8. Admission of children to hospital for reasons not based on clinical need.
9. Number of ear, nose and throat operations of questionable benefit and length of stay.
10. Generic prescribing and development of a joint formulary for both Health Authorities.

The six asterisked were dropped after evaluation.

The evaluation process involved using a weighting by criteria to be agreed. Not surprisingly, it was impossible to gain consensus on the weightings. However, the criteria were:

- effectiveness;
- distance from national target;
- numbers of patients treated;
- whether the intervention was centred on people;
- the severity of the condition;
- the extent of jurisdiction of the Health Authority.

Eventually nine recommendations went through into the next strategy document and contracts. In conclusion though, it was acknowledged that the whole process did involve making value judgements and having knowledge of the local circumstances.

In all cases investment decisions depend on finding sufficient resources. This list illustrates some different approaches used by various Authorities to find resources, either to meet further investments or to meet budget limitations.

- top slicing;
- reorganizing existing services;
- changing providers and/or gaining efficiency savings;
- new money or alternative funding sources (from capitation gains, health gain funds, private finance initiative, R&D projects, social services, private insurance);
- reviewing the need for certain treatments;
- locality purchasing models.

Real-life examples from Health Authorities around the country indicate the range of changes that are possible: some are allocating funds to a wider range of services in primary care, such as physiotherapy and counselling; some have been investing in developing GP practice premises and equipment by making use of funds for hospital and community health services as well as those for general medical services; still others have sought to negotiate improvements in access to secondary care services, eg through reduced waiting times. Many Health Authorities have supported the provision of consultant outreach clinics in primary care settings, bringing the hospital clinician's expertise into the local surgery. Some critics, however, feel that this is not a cost-effective use of consultants' time.

In some areas Health Authorities have chosen to purchase selected services, such as vasectomy, from accredited practices instead of hospitals. Improvements in priority services, such as mental health, have been achieved by aligning these services more closely with general practice. Other Health Authorities have been working with local authorities on joint commissioning of health and social care, often involving other services like housing.

Looking looking back at Figure 5.5, there are really three mechanisms for achieving change and, hopefully, getting more value for money.

The first is prevention of admission, which could include more community care of the sick, eg hospital at home schemes and GP beds in community hospitals; or more out-patient and day case investigations and treatment, including day case surgery.

The second is earlier discharge, for example by reduced length of stay due to improved techniques like surgery or prophylactic use of antibiotics, improved discharge policies or improved community based convalescent facilities, eg part of the hospital at home schemes.

The third is reduced attendance at hospital. This could be achieved by a reduction in GP referrals through using guidelines and stricter criteria; less out-patient follow-ups by hospital due to more GP follow-ups of patients; more GP chronic disease management clinics, for example in asthma and diabetes; and by carrying out more hospital type procedures in general practice, eg sigmoidoscopy, minor surgery.

All these examples revolve around stopping or reducing some

activities in the hospital setting and starting or increasing the activities carried out in general practice.

From a practical and pragmatic point of view, the following questions may be useful in trying to decide which mix of services and location is best for patients and their carers and which is the most cost-effective option.

- What should we do more of, or better?
- What should we do less of, or stop?
- What should we start to do?
- What should we continue to do as now?

While it may seem simple, it has been used with groups of GPs who have found it valuable in sharing insights and perspectives in the way services could be developed.

Rationing is a thorny area – different levels of rationing occur both nationally and locally. It is not possible to reduce the process of allocating resources to just a technical exercise – it involves making value judgements. There are a number of different techniques and approaches, as illustrated, and even simple ones can be effective. It also helps to look at rationing in terms of bite-sized chunks.

Accusations are often made of the Health Service that there is plenty of data around, but very little useful information. In order for us to undertake effective decision making we need information on the size of the problem (HNA), the availability and costs of interventions and the expected and actual benefits for patients (in terms of health gain and outcomes). It is in these areas that the results of clinical and economic evaluations are needed. However, the existence of such information is usually insufficient to bring about a change in policy or clinical management. It requires the wide dissemination of such evidence and, often, a marketing approach to convince managers and clinicians of the validity of the evidence to support a change in patient management.

To balance the information from clinical and economic evaluation, the government has encouraged commissioners to become 'champions of the people' and to plan and deliver services that are responsive to local need, identified by epidemiological approaches. Just as important are the perceived needs of individuals and communities.

The active involvement of the public in decision making has

been carried out in a variety of ways. The principles that indicate the cost-effectiveness and usefulness of such activities are those which:

- are amenable to public debate;
- make possible a genuine change in the service provided;
- are not subject to rigid guidelines or targets from the centre.

Many methods are documented elsewhere for generating useful information from the local population. Public confidence will occur where views are demonstrably included in decision making. There is no value or positive outcome for consultation over communication when only one course of action is really feasible.

Step 3. Action Plans

Having chosen targets for health gain, the third part of the process is, as we have seen with our original planning questions, generating action plans. The content of each action plan will vary according to the nature of the topic chosen and the targets that have been set. The process for managing action plans has already been described, as has the process of implementing the plan itself, so in this section, we are looking at the clinical approach.

The Clinical Approach

A number of techniques and approaches exist to help those involved in developing action plans. Through them we can identify the most suitable approach for each disease area. For example, the plan may make use of guidelines for patient or disease management, processes for running health promotion and chronic disease management clinics and disease prevention initiatives. The model shown in Figure 5.5 matches 'paths of causality' with examples of responses.

There are a number of diseases for which the DoH has mapped out the specific appropriate interventions and these are becoming widely published within the NHS and Audit Commission reports.

Using Guidelines for Better Healthcare

Once a model has been drawn up it is easier to develop guidelines, which are really clinical action plans. There has been much discussion in the NHS and the media on the content and value of guidelines in the management of medical conditions. As a consequence, we have seen the development of guidelines in both primary care and the hospital setting.

The move towards the development of guidelines has largely been driven by, first, the purchaser/provider arrangement and the interest in the content of contracts between commissioners or fundholders and Trusts; second, by the current interest in evidence based decision making and evidence based practice, which is receiving greater attention currently, given the application of managed care models in the UK; and third, through the quality agenda, also receiving greater attention now through audit activities and the content of executive letters, particularly the ones dealing with clinical effectiveness.

The quality agenda in the NHS is characterized by:

- a desire to improve standards of care (towards best care);
- a move away from activity measures to outcome measures;
- activities by the Royal Colleges and professional groupings, eg BTS guidelines on asthma;
- Patients' Charter and increasing consumer involvement in healthcare choices;
- a desire for improved communication between primary and secondary care – seamless service, incorporating referral and discharge plans;
- calls for decision making based on effectiveness, efficiency and appropriateness;
- a wish for clarification of roles and accountabilities within the clinical community.

Benefits of guidelines

Different groups benefit from the creation and use of guidelines.

1. Healthcare professionals benefit because by sticking to guidelines, except for individual cases, variation between individual clinicians is reduced. Guidelines are a way to show that clinical decisions are made more explicit on the basis of

evidence. With a number of clinicians using the same framework, common practice between professionals generates trust; and target setting and monitoring by peers is made easier in both primary and secondary care. As an additional bonus, quality management in primary care should reduce the demand on emergency services in secondary care. Finally, if guidelines are created that are workable and represent best practice, there is increased cost-effective use of both financial and human resources.

2. The benefits of guidelines are also clear for NHS management. By being sure that the guidelines represent good practice and can be used for the majority of patients managers can plan the use of finite resources more easily. By encouraging the use of guidelines they should be able to ensure increased cost-effective use of NHS resources. It will also help in target setting and monitoring at Health Authority and Health Board level. In the longer term guidelines may also save overall costs for the NHS, by allowing purchasers to disinvest in inappropriate or ineffective care and allowing reinvestment in alternative areas where most health gain can be achieved.

3. For patients, the benefits can be seen as improved confidence in consistent levels of care. This is important, as often the most visible part of the process – the way in which patients are cared for – is the one that inspires confidence in patients. Again, in the longer term, patients should have better quality of life – reductions in mortality and morbidity, and reductions in unnecessary duplications of management procedures (eg X-rays and other diagnostic tests). As the emphasis in the NHS is now on responding to patients' needs and making services more appropriate for them, it is likely that much more care can be provided for them at or close to their homes.

Content
A gold standard set of guidelines might contain information and recommendations in the following areas:

- the disease itself;
- costs of disease;
- health needs assessment;
- target setting guidelines;
- treatments/algorithms/non-intervention management;

- management guidelines;
- audit guidelines;
- a description of patient education and management of AIDS.

Recommendations based on evidence, or expert opinion, will be labelled according to the strength of supporting evidence. As we saw earlier, there is a growing support infrastructure within the NHS, particularly in the area of research and development, which is designed to support the evidence base that can be incorporated into guidelines. There is also a lot of support within the medical community for national development of guidelines that could be adapted locally.

Cautionary notes

There are a few downsides to guidelines, and it is worth being aware of them before spending effort on what might, ultimately, be a dissatisfying activity. In the first instance, formalized protocols may constrain clinical freedom or stifle innovation – perhaps 'fossilizing' clinical practice. This would not be helpful in an era of technological evolution. If guidelines do become stagnant they may become out of date – not merely out of fashion – meaning that patients are put at risk by being given suboptimal treatment.

The second point to note is that some guidelines may have been developed in the hope of reducing costs, rather than being focused on quality. As mentioned before, the process of developing and implementing guidelines is time-consuming, demanding significant drive and commitment from all involved. So guidelines that are created simply to make cost savings may also compromise the quality of patient care.

If guidelines are deficient is some way they may not be completed or used. Some guidelines may lack credibility if they have been poorly presented or are based on inaccurate, out-of-date information. So a quality check is needed to make sure that the guidelines that are created are robust.

Recipe for Success in Creating Guidelines

In a recent report on the use and usefulness of guidelines, a number of rules for success were spelt out.

1. The creation and use of guidelines will only be worthwhile if they reduce the felt pressure on practitioners and are immediately seen as doing so. In this case clinicians should experience less 'interference' from others in their clinical practice.
2. Designers of guidelines must realize guidelines may have side-effects, so they must be aware of the full situation in which they will be used.

   There will be consequences, both for patients and the full clinical teams who adopt the guidelines as their regular practice. This may require changes in procedures, which should be recognized and allowed for.
3. Guidelines should be short, clear and dogmatic.
4. Guidelines must make it clear that practitioners are free to use clinical judgement in the light of an individual patient's condition. A guideline is just that – a guideline – not a protocol that is unbending and inflexible. Not all patients will fit the criteria necessary for the use of the guideline and allowances should be made for this.
5. Where appropriate it should be made clear that what is offered is a model, offered to help design a guideline to meet specific requirements. Although it may be tempting to adopt a guideline completely, it is likely that there will be particular local circumstances that mean modifications are needed.
6. Wherever possible a flow chart should be given in addition to the text. It would be a clear advantage if text and chart were on facing pages. The flow chart should improve understanding and the clarity of the advice being given.
7. Guidelines should contain a statement of objectives and intended readership. Different aspects of patient management may be appropriate for different members of the clinical team.
8. Guidelines should contain advice to patients on what to expect and watch out for. If there is something written that patients can take away and read by themselves, or have talked through with them by a member of the clinical team, eg a practice nurse, it is likely that they will comply better with the recommended treatment and the chances of success are better.

In developing guidelines, therefore, we should remember that they need to be owned locally and not be perceived as being inferior to those published by national bodies. It is important that they are updated regularly and not allowed to stagnate. It is important to ensure that guidelines are responsive to changes in thinking on the management of disease and incorporate innovations in treatment. Even more importantly, they should be effectively disseminated and used by the appropriate readership.

Setting priorities

It would make sense, in the light of what we have already covered, for local guideline development to be determined for areas of local need, so, that way clinicians are working with others on the local health strategy. Another area to consider is where rigorous national guidelines exist. This makes adoption of good practice easier. It is useful also to consider this where current practice diverges from best practice, as using guidelines here will provide the potential for significant health gain.

Implementation

'Guidelines are more likely to be effective if they take into account local circumstances, are disseminated by an active educational intervention, and implemented by patient specific reminders relating directly to professional activity.' (*Effective Healthcare Bulletin*, 1994)

Once guidelines exist, there can be incentives and penalties for enforcing adoption. For example, in the US, doctors are faced with rigorous protocols of managed care, which they have to follow for reimbursement. In this case, financial reward is the driver for change, together with a wish to practise good medicine and, a particular aspect of medical practice in the US, a wish to avoid claims for medical negligence. While this is not yet common in the UK, there is a logic for adopting good practice to minimize the risk. It is not just a clinical issue, but a serious one for managers. There is an increase in the number of risk management experts who advise and guide providers in this difficult area.

The most powerful part of the implementation strategy in the adoption of guidelines is behaviour during the consultation, so it is useful to think about ways in which clinicians can be encouraged to follow the guidelines. There is some evidence on the effectiveness of different educational and implementational strategies. We look at changing behaviour in more detail in Chapter 8, so it is enough to say here that changes in behaviour are difficult to initiate, foster and maintain. Yet it is this aspect of the guidelines' initiative that will determine whether they succeed or fail.

Chances of success can be improved by looking at the quality dimension. By linking a range of quality initiatives a set of action plans can be worked out.

The NHS R&D initiatives will define appropriate practice that will be translated into guidelines, perhaps built into contracts, and audit will monitor adherence to guidelines. Although this process is irrefutably logical and objective, experience over the last few years has shown that the naturally conservative UK clinician views guideline creation and use with a healthy scepticism. Despite the increasing wealth of evidence, knowledge of individual patients often remains subjective. It is this reliance on individual clinical judgement that has sustained generations of practising clinicians. It is important not to lose this and push for what has been called 'cook book medicine'. Ultimately there must be a balance between evidence based decision making and the judgement of individual doctors treating individual patients.

Several models have been developed to assist in the successful management of change, some of which have been supplied to various aspects of the NHS, including guideline creation and use. No single strategy overcomes barriers to change. A variety of methods is required in combination to implement new ideas successfully.

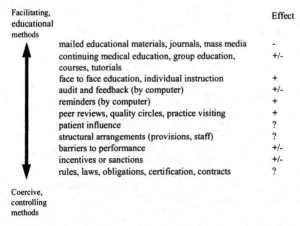

Facilitating, educational methods	Effect
mailed educational materials, journals, mass media	-
continuing medical education, group education, courses, tutorials	+/-
face to face education, individual instruction	+
audit and feedback (by computer)	+/-
reminders (by computer)	+
peer reviews, quality circles, practice visiting	+
patient influence	?
structural arrangements (provisions, staff)	?
barriers to performance	+/-
incentives or sanctions	+/-
rules, laws, obligations, certification, contracts	?

Coercive, controlling methods

Figure 5.7 Effectiveness of intervention designed to change routines in general practice (Grol, 1993)

Wider use of guidelines

Once guidelines have been developed they can be used as a valuable element in resource allocation decisions. Even where guidelines are adopted and used, questions remain as to their role here. It is generally accepted that guidelines can inform decisions on resource allocation, but are only one of a number of factors that need to be taken into account. Other factors including the setting of priorities and, of course, the patient's choice.

Guidelines also have a key part to play in the cycle to improve clinical effectiveness. Scotland has done some leading-edge work in this area, through the activities of the groups SNAP (Scottish Needs Assessment for Purchasing), CRAG (Clinical Research and Audit Group) and SIGN (Scottish Intercollegiate Guidelines Network), as shown in Figure 5.8.

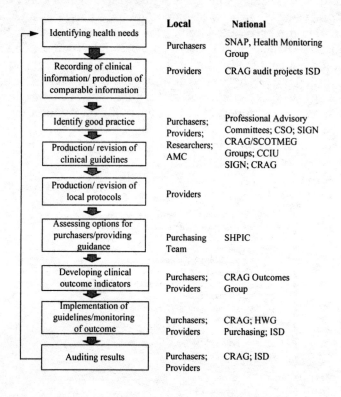

	Local	National
Identifying health needs	Purchasers	SNAP, Health Monitoring Group
Recording of clinical information/ production of comparable information	Providers	CRAG audit projects ISD
Identify good practice	Purchasers; Providers; Researchers; AMC	Professional Advisory Committees; CSO; SIGN CRAG/SCOTMEG Groups; CCIU SIGN; CRAG
Production/ revision of clinical guidelines		
Production/ revision of local protocols	Providers	
Assessing options for purchasers/providing guidance	Purchasing Team	SHPIC
Developing clinical outcome indicators	Purchasers; Providers	CRAG Outcomes Group
Implementation of guidelines/monitoring of outcome	Purchasers; Providers	CRAG; HWG Purchasing; ISD
Auditing results	Purchasers; Providers	CRAG; ISD

Figure 5.8 Assessing clinical effectiveness (note that purchasers include GP fundholders and providers include primary care providers)

The national bodies mentioned here do not necessarily exist in the same form in other parts of the UK, but there are professional and clinical organizations that have the remit and responsibility for the different tasks outlined in the chart.

On balance, guidelines have a great contribution to make in improving standards of care for patients. Their use, in both primary and secondary care, and across the interface, is increasing. The trend in guideline development has seen a shift away from consensus based guidelines towards evidence based guidelines. These offer a sounder basis than in the past for decision making that extends beyond clinical practice to resource allocation. However, we must remember that there is still a place for individual clinical judgement, where doctors respond subjectively and explicitly to the needs of the individual patient.

Managed Care

'The NHS is one of the first and most successfully managed healthcare systems in the world.' (Hatcher, 1995)

There has been a huge interest in the area of managed care in the UK, largely driven by developments in the US. Managed care in this context is defined as 'systematic intervention by healthcare commissioners in the management of health services provided to a defined population to improve health status and improve health access, efficiency and efficacy'. There are a number of structural and functional indicators that define managed care as it works in the UK. Not all measures are in place everywhere, but there are enough examples to at least indicate the direction of the trend and its applicability.

The structural elements required for managed care are:

- Limiting consumer choice of primary care provider to an approved list. In the UK this means a local GP with an open list.
- Using a primary care gatekeeper to control access to secondary care. The GP contract requires 24-hour cover by GPs to prevent unnecessary expensive Accident and Emergency activity. Preauthorization is covered by the purchaser/provider contract or by extra contractual arrangements.

- Selective contracting between purchasers and providers to gain advantage by purchasers. In the UK the Health Authority regulates FHS spend and the arrangements between purchasers and providers for acute and community services.
- Using financial incentives for primary care providers. GPs are paid by weighted capitation and bonuses for immunization/screening targets, etc. GP fundholders can keep savings. NB Weighted capitation discourages risk selection of patients, biased against complex, costly cases.

The functional dimensions are:

- Utilization management. Primary care doctor profiling and use of care pathways, shared care guidelines and case-mix groups based on length of stay information to control resource utilization. Referral and prescribing practice profiles are used for resource allocation in primary care.
- Quality management. There is a drive towards this in the UK, as we discuss elsewhere. Professional credentialling (eg re-accreditation) is a facet of this.

By observing which of these are already well established, organizations can decide where development work is needed to implement a fully fledged managed care environment. One organization that has already put this into place, throughout their provider organizations, is BUPA.

Step 4. Monitoring Results

A number of methods are available for determining the results of healthcare interventions on patients. One of the most useful, apart from the clinical trials we looked at earlier, is medical or clinical audit.

> 'Medical audit is the systematic critical analysis of the quality of medical care, including the procedures for diagnosis and treatment, the use of resources and the resulting outcome and quality of life for the patient.' (DoH, 1990)

The Seven Step Audit Approach

This approach is useful for all types of professional audit, whether primary or secondary care, unidisciplinary or multi-disciplinary in scope.

1. Design the audit This stage involves selecting which subjects are most suitable for audit. Here, too, you can clarify the audit objectives and what you would like it to achieve. Tasks can be shared out around the team and you can decide which patients you wish to collect information on.

2. Decide criteria and agree standards This is where you decide what is going to be measured and what you will accept as a standard for care. These will be influenced by what data are available and how the data are to be collected. You could look at physiological status, clinical indices such as mortality, complication rates, readmission rates, social activity and days off work or school.

3. Collect and organize data There are a number of ways of doing this, eg retrospectively or prospectively. You can look through patient case notes and compare them to the indicators already chosen. There may be other records, questionnaires or patient surveys that you can use to find information.

4. Analyse audit data The next step is to make some sense of the data you have collected. The information can be matched against the standards set before and this will show where the activities and outcomes match, or do not match clinical needs and best practice in patient management.

5. Identify cause of non-achievement Once the view is reached that current practice does not meet expected practice, you can look for reasons why this is the case. Then action plans can be devised to address them.

6. Implement changes This is where the action plans are put into effect.

7. Monitor progress   This is the final part of the process, which should show that the action plan has addressed the problem. Then another topic can be agreed for the next audit!

The aim of audit is to improve patient care by monitoring the whole treatment process – from the moment the patient walks through the door of their local pharmacy to the end of their treatment, whether that takes place in their GP's surgery, at home or in hospital. Audit should improve efficiency and standards within a practice as well as in the wider healthcare context.

Background

Until audit became part of mainstream medical practice there was no systematic way to measure the quality of service delivered to patients and compare it with the care given by different practices or in different parts of the country. With no nationally agreed standards of care individual practices and hospitals had no idea if the service they delivered compared well with that of their colleagues elsewhere.

Making the audit process work has been largely left to the medical and allied professions and the focus has been on introducing a system of educational peer review.

Cooperation within the medical profession is fundamental to the success of the auditing process and the Royal Colleges have given audit a high priority. They have given advice to the Clinical Standards Advisory Group, which helps formulate generally agreed standards of care, and have also issued publications resulting from conferences involving all parts of the medical profession.

Funds have been provided by DoH to assist with the implementation of audit. These funds are passed to providers by purchasers, who are therefore in a good position to ensure that clinical practice improves.

Getting Started

The aim of audit is to maintain and encourage good standards of care and improve on poor standards for the benefit of patients. One of the first tasks for those involved in audit is the setting of agreed standards for patient care. This step is important because these standards will form the criteria against which individual patient care can be measured. While it is possible to set quite specific standards in some areas, for example a reduction in the number of patients needing readmission within 30 days of discharge from 5 per cent to 2 per cent within 12 months, in other areas setting such tight standards may be more difficult. In these situations, we can look at a more flexible system – perhaps ranging on a scale from 'ideal' or 'optimum' to 'reasonable' or 'minimum'. It is a good idea to choose standards that reflect the needs of the local population and their special health requirements.

Once the standards have been set and agreed, it will be easier to compare the patient care delivered by individual practices or teams. If, for some reason, the comparison shows differences between practices or between what is currently practised and the set standards, then the practice or team can check to see what reasons there might be for the differences. In this way specific advice can be given to practices that have difficulties in achieving the standards in certain areas of healthcare. If the advice is sound and the practice or team wishes to change its methods of working they can involve the whole healthcare team in adapting to different behaviours. Hopefully, this will mean that positive actions are taken by the team and optimum outcomes for patients are achievable.

The whole idea of audit may seem daunting, so the 'bite-sized chunk' idea can work well here, too. Audit does not have to apply to every patient or every procedure that the healthcare team carry out. In fact, experience shows that it is better to limit the scope of audit early on and so make it easier to achieve worthwhile results, which helps both in feedback and for wider adoption. It then becomes more straightforward to extend the scope of the audits done and the complexity of the subjects that are tackled.

Using the Results

One of the benefits of audit is that it encourages healthcare professionals to update their practice. This includes their knowledge of diagnostic techniques, methods of monitoring diseases and their treatment and any therapeutic advances that may be introduced over time. Audit is also good for improving processes and in developing best practice guidelines for the treatment of patients. This also helps doctors in keeping up to date with the latest evidence – a part of their postgraduate training and a way to make best use of the research and development work being carried out not only across the UK, but around the world. One of the great things about audit is that it is a process of self-examination and anyone can identify where further information or education would be of help.

If common areas are identified where further education would be beneficial, then postgraduate deans can build these topics into update programmes. Many professional groups are interested in this area, so managers can help by making the communication links between all the different groups work well. It may be that groups would benefit from updating on the techniques available for audit themselves, so that the latest thinking on audit is shared around the clinical community. The sorts of areas that can be covered in such a programme could include management techniques to monitor feedback on performance and implementing changes to patient care.

Benefits of Audit in Clinical Practice

If audit results generate better information on outcomes and those can be related to the process of care that patients experience, that will add greatly to the body of evidence for best practice. It could also improve the understanding that patients have of the care that is being given to them, or that is available through their local practices and in hospital. As we said before, audit is mainly an educational activity, so it should contribute to the personal professional development of all health professionals who take part. Part of audit is in recording what is done; in this way it can help with justification of clinical care and making sure that resources are used effectively. Audit is a fundamental part of the planning process when applied to clinical settings, so it is a part of good management and clinical practice. It is also a useful way of showing the public that quality activity is being carried out. There is also the possibility that audit will become an increasingly important part of defence in justifying treatment where there may be disputes or litigation.

Critical Success Factors in Audit

A number of factors need to be taken into account in order for audit to succeed. The first is getting all the people on board, clinical and allied professions as well as management. Audit should be carried out in an atmosphere of participation, consultation, trust and support. The second is making sure there is enough time. All audit activities should be carried out as part of normal working practice. This may be quite difficult for small practices whose resources are stretched, but pooling expertise and support can help overcome this.

In order to carry out effective audits support and training are required for everyone taking part. Knowing what to measure and how to measure it can save wasted effort at a later stage. Finally, with the advent of computers, it should be easier to carry out audit. There are, however, concerns with confidentiality of data, so safeguards should be in place to ensure that individual patients cannot be identified.

The basic principle of audit is that it should improve patient care by comparing what is done against agreed best practice (a standard) and identify and resolve problems that may crop up in caring for patients. In order for this to happen effectively the whole team must be committed to audit. If everyone is involved in designing the audit in the first place they are more likely to carry out the subsequent audit activities.

What to Audit?

In taking this decision you may like to think of the five main needs of primary prevention and secondary control which work as a general principle:

1. immunization and screening.
2. exclusion of illness.
3. early diagnosis.
4. management of acute and chronic disease (including psychiatric and psychosocial distress).
5. terminal care.

These are all needs where there are recognizable medical interventions and processes and for which there are recognized outcomes (ie the effects on the patient). These interventions and outcomes are measurable.

So, in summary, suitable subjects for audit are those where patients have said they consider them to be important, where there are recognized medical processes of care and where there are clear and measurable outcomes.

The following are suggestions for suitable audit topics.

Disease and conditions
Hypertension, dyspepsia management, care of chronic alcoholics, care of the elderly, diabetes, thyroid, asthma, chronic disease management, migraine, UTIs in children, management of upper GI symptoms and acute disease management.

Practice and interface management
Patient records, prescribing (including repeat prescribing), appointment times, referrals, home visits after hospital discharge, therapeutics, patient satisfaction, emergency calls.

Prevention and clinics
Contraception, hepatitis vaccination, shared care obstetrics, breastfeeding rates, coronary heart disease clinics, health promotion clinics and well-person clinics.

Implementing Change

To be useful, audit should not only analyse medical care but also identify areas for improvement and involve a commitment to address shortcomings. So, audit involves change – in clinical procedures, practice and clinical team management and, as I have mentioned before, changes in the attitudes and behaviour of members of the clinical team.

The objective of the change is to improve quality and the RCGP have put forward a list of quality outcomes to help:

- the prevention of disease, or control of the disease process;
- improvement or preservation of the patient's level of function in the family, at work or in social activities;
- relief of the patient's symptoms, distress and anxiety, and avoidance of iatrogenic (drug induced) symptoms;
- prevention of premature death;
- minimizing the cost of the illness to the patient and family;

- giving the patient satisfaction with the care provided;
- relieving, or at least clarifying, the patient's interpersonal problems;
- preserving the integrity of the patient from an ethical point of view.

Change can be perceived as a threat, which in turn may cause tension and resistance. Doing something differently can be seen as a questioning of competence, a risk to status or a criticism of what went before. So it is important to get the proposed change viewed as an opportunity rather than as a threat. If it works well, learning to deal with change can bring positive benefits – greater creativity, better performance and increased achievement.

Example – Auditing Referrals

GPs, in their role as gatekeepers to secondary care and, in the case of fundholders or commissioning groups, as purchasers, are responsible for assessing the need for many hospital services. Since April 1990, they have been required to provide information on the number of patients referred to hospital. This makes auditing referrals a useful area to look at. Tackling this is one way to estimate the progress of the move in the NHS towards a primary care led NHS and the shift from secondary to primary care where, currently, 90 per cent of episodes of ill health are dealt with.

In an ideal world patients would be treated in, or close to, their own homes. In many cases the community offers the most cost-effective approach to managing patients. However, there are cases where referral is the most appropriate approach to take. Knowing when to refer can be difficult. A number of studies in recent years have shown up to a fourfold variation in the rates of referral between GPs. Reducing clinical variation of this type is one of the current NHS priorities. By monitoring the processes and outcomes of referral through audit, a greater understanding of why these variations occur and how to manage patients more effectively, while making better use of NHS resources, will generate better outcomes.

Audit is a useful method to investigate both clinical reasons for referral and guidelines of care in referring patients between primary and secondary care.

The benefits of doing this audit could be to:

- minimize unnecessary referrals, with associated reduction in inconvenience for patients and their families and carers;
- agree management plans and treatment guidelines between general practice and secondary care to provide best possible patient care;
- agree the content of GP and hospital referral and discharge letters;
- agree the criteria for admission and discharge of patients.

Any of these could be used as the objectives for the audit – step 1 in the seven step process.

Step 2 is deciding the criteria and agreeing the standards. Here are some suggested criteria and standards for this audit.

Criteria	Standards
(a) Patients	
Patients who require in-patient/out-patient services	Decrease
Community-based follow-up	Increase
Hospital acquired infection rates	Decrease
Ratio of day-case to in-patients	Increase
Readmission within X days	Decrease
Appropriate communication with patients by all staff	%
No booked admissions sent home without treatment	%
(b) Content of referral letter to hospital/consultant	
1. Date of birth	100%
2. Presenting history	
3. Past relevant history	
4. Family history	
5. Drug abuse	
6. Present medication	
7. Allergies	
8. Investigations – abnormal results only	
9. Clinical findings	
10. Reason for referral	
(c) Referral and treatment guidelines	
Develop guidelines between primary and secondary care	%

Joint referral decisions by doctor and patient   %

(d) Content of referral letters from hospitals

Diagnostic and treatment information to be included 100%
Management plan for each patient   100%
Replies to GPs queries   100%

(e) Communication between primary and
      secondary care

Discharge slips to be received within one week   100%
List of each department's available services to be   100%
    sent to GPs
GPs to be sent monthly updates on waiting times   100%

Step 3 – Collecting and organizing data (see p.99)

Step 4 – Analysing the audit data (see p.99)

Step 5 – Identifying causes of non-achievement (see p.99)
There may be a number of reasons why the agreed standards
have not been met. These could include:

- no guidelines in place between the practice and hospital;
- reason for referral is not agreed and understood by both the
  practice and hospital;
- patient notes are incomplete and/or referral letters contain
  incomplete information.

Step 6 – Implementing the change
The following suggestions may assist with changing practice in
referrals.

- Use a checklist to write a referral letter to the hospital. This
  will ensure that all appropriate information is included,
  particularly the reason for the referral.
- Develop referral guidelines between general practice and hospital.
- Ensure that appropriate referrals are made with regard to the
  length of waiting times and those referred.
- Ask the hospital team to suggest alternative referral sources if
  the wait is too long.

- Ask the hospital team for advice on management while awaiting the procedure.

Particular issues may come up that are regarded as requiring speedy treatment, but referring patients from primary care and back again is expensive. If it is done appropriately, it is justified, but if badly, then it is a waste of resources. It is therefore appropriate to study referrals for effectiveness and efficiency, in addition to judging them on the basis of health need.

Step 7 – Monitoring progress (see p.100)

Performance Management

Performance management includes the methods available for measuring the process of clinical practice and the possible outcomes for patients, but also covers other, more managerial aspects of health service activity. By examining different aspects of health service management it is possible to establish effective working practices.

Performance management is relevant at both an individual and a corporate level. As with the planning process in total, it is important that individuals within the organization have a mission and set of values to work to. These give them a sense of what they are being measured against. Management by objectives is one technique to assess performance. Another book in this series, *Performance Management and Appraisal in Health Services*, describes this area in much more detail. So here is only an outline of the strategies for performance management.

1. Specify performance requirements.
2. Design jobs and functions.
3. Develop organizational capability and culture.
4. Develop staff.
5. Provide rewards.

The design and implementation of these strategies is the job of the top management team and the human resources department. Expert support for the implementation of these strategies will ensure the organization is in a good position to survive in the future.

Chapter 6

Joint Planning and Collaboration with Social Services

This chapter explores the potential for collaboration, prompted by a primary care led NHS and a desire to look after patients in, or as near to, their homes as possible. I look at the developments in using the concept of 'care manager' in this setting and the benefits that brings, both to patients and their families and friends, and to the Health Service and Social Services teams.

When the purchaser/provider split came into being in 1991 the Health Service world used the phrase 'joint purchasing' to explain the activities of district Health Authorities working jointly with GP fundholders to determine purchasing plans for the area. Latterly 'joint commissioning' has been used to describe the addition of non-fundholding GPs in the planning and monitoring of secondary and community care services. The latest development in this field has been to involve Social Services in this process, to cater for the range of patient needs that lie outside those traditionally met by the NHS.

There are a number of advantages to including the Social Services dimension to NHS activities. For example, the concept of a mixed economy has been pushed further forward in the field of Social Services – where purchasers exercise choice in providers, using both private and voluntary sectors in addition to Local Authority run services. In the healthcare field, this is less well developed, although fundholders have used their purchasing power in a similar way, for example to reduce waiting lists for elective procedures. Private hospitals have won contracts from fundholders to clear waiting lists and this is one of the factors that has led to the fundholding scheme being accused of engendering 'two-tierism' in the system. We are now seeing Health Authorities using private providers for the same reasons. Patients are encouraged to view this positively, for example through the assurances that many of the clinicians are those who the patient would have seen if the service had been provided by a Trust provider.

Another area in which social care has advanced further than Health Service activities is in the 'cost per case' contract model. Individualized care for patients and the use of 'care managers' to coordinate the service response ensures a 'patient-focused' approach. More about care managers in a moment.

In the past the grey area between health and social needs could result in patients not receiving services while the red tape was sorted out. In addition there has been an ongoing debate about which service sector should 'own' the whole process, which can also hinder the implementation of 'care packages'. Care packages are plans for patients that describe the total care arrangements that an individual patient can expect to receive in the treatment process.

More recently, with the advent of means testing for social care provision, there are further barriers to effective patient centred approaches. What can seem a simple plan when decided and agreed by all the services involved can get complicated when the patient's 'share' of payment is calculated. However, there are some examples of best practice from around the country, which have attempted to get round the bureaucratic hurdles and have concentrated on delivering the most appropriate type of service possible within budgetary constraints.

Shared Vision and Strategy

A good starting point on the road to ensuring success of joint commissioning is that the authorities involved have a shared vision and strategy. If one is not already in place the process outlined in Chapter 2 can be used to develop one. Where one is already in place it may be helpful to review it and ensure, once it has been agreed, that it is communicated to all stakeholders. In that way one of the fundamental building blocks for the effective working relationship between the different agencies involved has been laid down. It can then be referred back to should there be any areas of disagreement in future.

A number of different types of initiatives have been put into place in an effort to target resources in the best way.

Role Clarity

First, by recognizing the statutory responsibilities of both health and Social Services agencies, the ground rules can be set. As we saw in Chapter 5, Health Authorities are responsible for identifying the health needs of their catchment area. In the same way, Local Authorities' Social Services departments are responsible for identifying the appropriate assessments of an individual's need for social care.

This involves a number of steps to ensure effective use of resources. The first part of this process is in assessing social care needs at a strategic level, which should be a shared strategy with other agencies; next, developing a strategy for allocating and applying resources to address the needs that are in line with locally developed social policies. Once the strategic objectives have been set the next step is in assessing individuals and planning their care in line with the agreed strategy in the same way as Health Authorities design purchasing plans for patients; further, Social Services will design and purchase packages of care tailored to meet the assessed needs of individuals and their carers. So, the first thing to get right is role clarity, between satisfying the health needs and the social needs.

This joint approach should ensure a more comprehensive assessment of need than can be tackled by each authority independently. Once the assessment has been carried out decisions can be taken on the most appropriate mix of services needed to deliver quality care. Following on from that the authorities involved should secure the delivery of services – not only, as in some cases, being the provider themselves (eg primary care services, in the case of GPs) but, more importantly, using their purchasing/commissioning role and contracting expertise to deliver appropriate, high quality services.

Care Manager

Once the statutory responsibilities have been established both commissioning bodies can work towards assuring those responsibilities. This is where a collaborative approach can pay dividends, rather than in the agencies continuing a somewhat sterile debate about ownership. This is increasingly important as patients are discharged earlier back to the community. For some patients the infrastructure of social care available in their home environment is a key determinant in helping them on the road to recovery. So, for example, the provision of home helps, meals on wheels and such like are needed at the point at which the patient returns home, and should be planned for even before the patient is admitted to hospital. In some parts of the country the role of 'care manager' has been introduced, to undertake the coordinating role across health and social care, in addition to ensuring all the healthcare aspects.

This will be valuable for those patients who benefit from one identifiable point of contact with a seemingly muddled system.

Project Manager

While the appointment of a care manager is one route to dealing with issues as seen from the patient's or carer's perspective, the successful implementation of joint commissioning from a cross-organizational perspective can be tackled by using a project manager or 'champion'. Their role is that of running the project – liaison between the agencies; getting objectives, tasks and deadlines agreed; progress chasing of those who have responsibilities within the project; monitoring progress of the project against objectives and evaluating the success of the project. Part of the role will revolve around the strategic aspects of joint commissioning, while the other part will be concerned with dealing with operational aspects.

Involving Users and Carers

An important principle in any commissioning activity is the involvement of users and carers. If they are involved in all stages they will be a 'sanity check' on the system, which will keep the process patient focused and minimize the bureaucracy referred to earlier.

Involvement should be with individuals and with representative groups. Patients and clients are represented by a number of organizations, eg Patients Association, Community Health Councils, Consumers Association, College of Health, Carers Association, voluntary organizations and others more directly involved in supporting patients with particular problems or diseases. Each will bring a different perspective to the joint commissioning process and it will be helpful to outline to each what they can expect from their contribution. For example, the right of veto may be part of the arrangement with some stakeholders and not others. Which groups have the right of veto will be important to clarify, so that expectations can be managed.

Many organizations and groups have undertaken consultation with users and carers. The most successful of the activities have been focus groups, where a specially invited group of participants (between 12 and 20 individuals) come together with a facilitator, often a locality manager, for discussion.

Evaluation of Success of Joint Commissioning

As with evaluation of the success of the business plan, the success of joint initiatives should be measured against the jointly agreed plan laid out at the start of the joint working arrangements. The same success criteria can then be applied. Of particular interest in this area is how the joint working arrangement addresses the requirements of efficiency, equity and choice for patients.

Some areas of healthcare provision have pioneered joint commissioning and useful lessons can be drawn from their successes and failures. One area that has probably done more than any other is mental health. So both healthcare and social care professionals can plan, based on experiences of such groups through the UK.

Chapter 7

Managing Stakeholders

Part of the planning process involves getting people (the stakeholders) on board in terms of their agreement with the plan. This is particularly the case where the plans address changes in the patterns of services to be purchased and provided. The stakeholders may themselves have a part to play, or may have a vested interest in the success or failure of the plan. This chapter looks at ways in which this process can be used to increase the chance of success for implementation of the plan.

> 'Top managers are like astronauts – to perform well, they need the intelligence that's back on the ground.' (Hamel and Prahalad, 1989)

Before stakeholders are identified it is probably a good idea to identify *why* they are important. Essentially, they are the only people who can define whether or not the plan and the organization are successful. It is therefore important, as project managers, both to recognize who they are, and ensure that they are involved to an appropriate degree in the plan and its execution. They will undoubtedly have a vested interest in the success or failure of the plan, so part of the stakeholder management process is to ensure that, whatever their view at the start of the planning process, they are either active supporters or, if against the plan at the start, are convinced that the plan as written is the right approach. The time taken for this, together with the diplomatic skills involved, cannot be underestimated!

Identifying Stakeholders

The first step in managing stakeholders is to identify the key people involved. As mentioned previously, this will include not only those involved in the planning phase, but also those involved in agreeing to and implementing the changes that may be necessary in order to achieve the objectives laid out in the plans. The list should include those people who are needed as resources for the plan and its implementation, those you need on your side, those who the plan is likely to affect and, lastly, those people who are not related to the plan, but who are watching with interest.

Stakeholders may be internal to the organization, or system, or external to it. Some aspects of managing stakeholders will be common to both, but there will be aspects that require a different approach, for example in identifying the benefits and risks associated with the consequences of decisions.

The following groups would be considered internal stake-holders for Health Authorities – GPs, dentists, pharmacists, opticians (although these are all independent contractors), staff, Board members. Internal stakeholders for Trusts would be – medical staff, nursing staff, allied professional staff (eg pharmacists), ancillary staff, management, contract staff, Board members.

External stakeholders for Health Authorities would be – local population, providers (Trusts, private providers and individuals), patients (as distinct from the local population), Local Authorities, NHS executive (including region), local voluntary organizations, local business suppliers, local employers, CHCs. External stakeholders for Trusts would include patient support groups, social services, probation service, CHC, NHS executive, general public, purchasers and other providers.

Assessing the Position of Stakeholders

A useful technique at this point is to draw a map. The first entry will be a list of the stakeholders, listed against the questions below. Having identified the people involved, an assessment is needed of whether or not they will support the plan or the changes that may result from it. Stakeholders can be grouped together according to their degree of support or otherwise for the plan and the organization. This will help significantly with the management strategy adopted in dealing with them throughout the planning process.

Useful Questions

Who wants you to succeed?	Who wants you to fail?
Who is betting on you to succeed?	Who is betting on you to fail?
Who is supporting you in public?	Who is supporting you in private?
Whose success affects you?	Whose success do you affect?
Who does your change benefit?	In what way does it benefit them?
Who does your change damage?	In what way does it damage them?
Who can your change happen without?	Who can your change not happen without?
Why can it not happen without them?	

This list is really for your personal use; some of the answers are not for sharing, other than with your core team. The important thing, though, is to have identified the *who, why* and *how* so that you can manage the introduction and implementation of the plan with the greatest chance of success.

Another way of looking at the involvement of different groups in the plan is to answer the following questions.

Who are the stakeholders?	What is their present involvement in the plan?
What future benefit is there in participating in the plan or its execution?	What are the potential costs to them of involvement?
What unaware 'wrecking power' do they have?	

This last question is designed to consider the 'What if...' question, that is, what is the worst that could happen if they were not involved or had not bought into the plan? How individuals use the power they have depends on whether the future benefit is seen to outweigh personal costs.

Managing the Stakeholders

How you approach stakeholders will depend on using the information from the answers to the previous questions. Some will require only progress reports on how the planning process is going; others will want to be involved in decision making. What you choose to tell them, or get them involved in, will determine the success or otherwise of the plan. By addressing their particular areas of interest and concerns, and by using any special expertise they may have, you stand a greater chance of success. The timing of these activities is also important, in making sure they are all comfortable with every step of the process.

It is important to understand the criteria by which the stakeholders are judging the plan – some suggestions of measures of success were laid out in Chapter 5. This will help in the important area of managing stakeholders' expectations as the planning process and its implementation move along. As a general point, expectations rarely match reality. What a plan can actually deliver is likely to be less than what is hoped for by the stakeholders. Some of the reasons for this were outlined when we looked at assumptions in Chapter 1 and in the modelling done for contingencies. Whatever the reason, if the stakeholders have an unrealistic expectation of the plan's outputs their confidence in the planning process will be eroded and they may be unwilling to participate or be consulted about plans in the future. It could also erode confidence in and of the planning team, if the process appears fraught with obstacles and demonstrates few successes. Even if the reality surpasses expectations, that needs managing; stakeholders will have higher expectations in the next round of the planning process. In that case it may not be possible for the next plan to deliver above that expectation and so we are back to the earlier state.

The job of the project leader here is to fit the reality of the plan to the success criteria mentioned earlier and then, by using effective communication, to keep stakeholders' expectations in line with reality during the life of the plan. The approach will depend on the level of involvement of the stakeholders. For example, there will be stakeholders who must be informed of any changes before the change happens; those who can be informed at the time of the change and, finally, those who can be told of the change after it has happened.

Chapter 8

Planning for Change

This chapter identifies techniques that are geared to improve quality in services, eg through the contracting process, quality initiatives and process re-engineering.

The 1990s are a time of unprecedented change for everyone in the NHS. The Health Service is faced with a number of new challenges, including:

- the need to match increasing patient and government expectations for health gain with limited resources;
- adapting to a managed healthcare system operating in an internal managed market;
- coordinating a multidisciplinary approach to patient care;
- evaluating performance on measurable patient outcomes;
- developing a focus on the patient as a customer.

Broad-based changes such as these require a multidisciplinary team approach, involving not only immediate colleagues but also others involved in running a department and caring for patients – in fact, anyone who can contribute to 'health gain' in a population. For example, there are greater pressures for increased cooperation between GP practices and hospitals due to the purchaser/provider split and the recognition of the benefits of providing seamless care for patients.

Speed of change is now *the* most critical issue for organizations to confront. Change is happening too quickly for organizations to select a set of objectives and adhere to them for an extended period of time; to leave the process of creating the vision of the organization to a single individual; or philosophize forever about their identity and where they are going. Organizations do not have to convince their staff about the fact of change; it is all around in every work-place. Organizations *do* have to give their staff confidence that they can survive and thrive.

To operate successfully in a changing environment, leaders of organizations need to concentrate on building an enduring organization – one that continues to provide products and services that are valued by those buying them – or, in the case of purchasers, one that purchases quality products and services. In addition, the organization is not satisfied with the status quo. It is continually looking to 'do things better' as well as 'doing better things'. Successful organizations are guided both by the results of what they do (in commercial terms this is profit maximization) but, more importantly, by the core values and a sense of purpose – hence the value of the mission statement. The set of core values will differ from organization to organization, ie there is no one 'right' set of values, but what is important is that the organization has a deep belief in them and should consistently live, breathe and express them in all it does. (See page 79 for more information on defining values).

Successful organizations show a powerful drive for progress, which enables them to change and adapt without compromising their ideals; they do not just talk about their core values, they are evident in the actions shown by the organization. People working in these organizations either fit in and thrive or leave, due to the all-pervasiveness of the dedication to the core values. Such organizations rely on in-house talent to generate change and ideas – they are not dependent on outsiders for fresh ideas and approaches. These organizations are not satisfied with goals; they tend to set audacious challenges to generate excitement and create strong forward momentum. They do not accept choices (this or that) but go for both or several options (this and that... and that!). Another characteristic of these organizations is that they focus primarily on improvement to beat themselves rather than the competition. They deliberately create discomfort with the status quo and thereby stimulate change and improvement before the external environment demands it. They make their best moves by experimentation, trial and error, opportunism and accident. They deliberately stimulate change and improvement.

Leaders of such organizations are committed, enthusiastic, and willing to share control. Charisma is not an essential ingredient; these leaders make a difference with actions, not words; they successfully create the feeling of self-control in their staff, which enables the organization to embrace the vision and move it forward.

Resistance to Change

Research reveals that ideas about implementing change in the Health Service can be naive, with strategies relying too heavily on published articles in medical journals or on lectures and group discussions. Whilst this is undoubtedly part of the process, it is not the whole story. The tendency to self-select reading matter and meetings may only serve to reinforce existing ideas. For example, there is evidence that only half of all GPs will attend meetings and then only on matters of specific interest to them. This makes it more difficult for them to pick up new ideas.

Resistance to change can stem from fear of the unknown, lack of information, threats to status, threats to established skills and competencies, fear of failure, reluctance to 'let go', lack of perceived benefits, threats to the power base, an organizational culture that is content to plod along without developing, history of previous custom, fear of looking stupid, feeling vulnerable and exposed, threat to self-esteem, loss of control of one's own destiny, loss of team relationships, high anxiety and stress.

To make changes, therefore, requires a cultural shift, a decision making shift for purchasers to practice/locality level, an activity shift (as discussed Chapter 5) and, finally, a financial shift (discussed in Chapter 6).

Change – Making it Happen

Several models have been developed to assist in the successful management of change, some of which have been applied to various aspects of the NHS.

Two key factors for success in managing change are a thorough analysis of the situation and effective buy-in by stakeholders. The latter requires effective meetings.

Situation analysis

1. Gather information from various sources, asking – has it been tried before?
2. Contact other people with similar initiatives and share information with the team – are we ready for change?
3. Research suggests that in industry innovations are more successful in organizations where there are spare resources – who makes the decisions?
4. Shared decision making is more likely to succeed – who are the key people?
5. Identify everyone involved in planning and implementing, or who is impacted by the changes (see the section on stakeholder management, Chapter 7). This builds ownership of, and commitment to the project – who might support the change?
6. Identify stakeholders and meet them individually to win their commitment – where do I go next?
7. Evaluate the feasibility of the proposed innovation and decide how to progress.

There are a number of techniques that can assist in the situation analysis part of the process. We covered the questions to ask in the previous chapter on managing stakeholders. Undertaking this type of analysis is powerful, in that it allows us to explore the costs and benefits of change, together with each person's power to promote or obstruct the process. How individuals use their power depends on whether the future benefit is seen to outweigh personal costs and the discomfort of the change proposed, ie:

$$C = (ABD) > X$$

where:
C = change; A = dissatisfaction with the status quo;
B = desirability of proposed change; D = practicability of change; X = cost of changing.

Another useful visual aid is the change star, which provides the four basic rules of communicating change:

- Tell them why – explain the business case, encourage criticism (repeating the objectives and benefits), involve others in the change.
- Make it manageable – anticipate impact of change on staff/patients, establish breathing space, break into small chunks, monitor and maintain momentum.
- Share the change – avoid 'announcementitis', share ownership of the change, talk about change face to face.
- Reinforce team and individual identity – adopt a 'people matter' style, reinforce success, create winners not losers, encourage team identity.

Effective buy-in from stakeholders – communicating new ideas

The method of communicating new ideas, and new information in general, is therefore critical. A number of steps must be taken:

1. Orientation – to generate awareness of and interest in the new ideas.
2. Insight – to understand the purpose of the ideas and how they address current weaknesses.
3. Acceptance – creating a positive commitment to the ideas and an intention to change and succeed.
4. Change – methods to implement the ideas and achieve positive outcomes.

A key part of involving and persuading stakeholders is to run effective meetings, paying attention to the points listed above. The membership of the meeting should include all stakeholders, who will have been approached individually prior to the meeting, to minimize the chance of a 'wrecking' manoeuvre. In common with all decision making meetings, the chair has a key role to play, in ensuring that

- contributions from all participants are recognized;
- contributions are elicited from all participants;
- no one person or group dominates the discussion;
- any points of disagreement or tension are identified and arbitrated;
- any personal attacks on participants are defused by refocusing the accusation on the problem and not the participant.

Meetings should have clear aims and an agenda. The length of the meeting should be agreed and adhered to.

To reach agreement, an honest response to the plan must be obtained from each member of the group. A useful technique is to ask each person the following three questions:

1. What appeals to you about this proposal now?
2. What concerns you about it now?
3. Do you need any more information to reach a decision?

Time should be allowed at the end of the meeting to:

- confirm what has been agreed;
- identify any remaining disagreements;
- decide what steps are needed to resolve them;
- set the date of the next meeting.

Meetings should be minuted (listing agreed actions, dates and responsibilities – an action plan) and the minutes should be circulated as soon as possible after the meeting.

CHECKLIST
to assess Health Authorities' ability
to manage the pace of change

1. Does the Authority have coherent policies driven by broad impressive visions?
2. Has the Authority policies built around minutely detailed blueprints?
3. Does the Authority have a management team with complementary skills, eg technical skills and political fixers (keeping contractors happy, handling Health Authority board members)?
4. Does the Authority foster a 'culture of panics' (financial and other crises every day)?
5. Does the Authority treat data seriously?
6. Does the Authority handle data efficiently?

7. Does the Authority work flexibly?
8. Does the Authority work through a formal hierarchy?
9. Do the managers enjoy a good relationship with clinicians?
10. Does the Authority have a cooperative network with other agencies (eg Local Authorities, other authorities in the NHS)?
11. Is the Authority developing cooperative networks with voluntary organizations?
12. Are the Authority's objectives clear and simply expressed?
13. Is the Authority good at prioritizing their objectives and workload?
14. Are managers persistent in pushing objectives?
15. Does the Authority share common boundaries with the Local Authority Social Services department?
16. Is the Authority able to form a dominant coalition with other powerful interests (eg fundholding groups)?
17. Does the Authority use short-term measures to meet financial targets?
18. Is the local political culture conducive to change?

If the organization is successful, the answers to the questions posed above would be:
1. Y 2. N 3. Y 4. N 5. Y 6. Y 7. Y 8. N 9. Y 10. Y 11. Y 12. Y 13. Y 14. Y 15. Y 16. Y 17. N 18. Y

The Contract

A contract is a bargain between two parties, whereby one party agrees or promises to do something in return for the promise of the other party to pay the price of those services.

The contract is one of the key mechanisms for generating quality improvements in the provision of NHS services. This section deals with the process, content and value of contracts in the pursuit of health gain.

Contracts in the NHS

There are generally three types of contract in the NHS – the corporate contract between purchasers, providers and the NHSE;

contracts between NHS purchasers and providers; and contracts between the NHS and private purchasers (eg for NHS pay beds) or private providers (eg for diagnostic or treatment services, or supplies). Some of the latter contracts are negotiated at a national level, eg that for provision of general medical services with GPs as independent contractors to the NHS. For most contracts, certain general principles apply, which I look at now.

The Scope of the Contract

The contract will include the price of the services to be provided, along with a description of those services. Virtually anything can be included in the contract as long as it is not unlawful or 'contrary to public policy'.

A description of the services (which may form a schedule to the main agreement) should therefore include not only the numbers of patients to be treated but also the agreed treatment regime and other services to be provided. For example, a contract could include the 'key indicators' used in the compilation of hospital league tables:

- Outpatient appointments. Percentage of patients seen within 30 minutes of appointment time.
- Day surgery. Percentage of elective episodes (planned and booked) by selected procedures for patients not requiring an overnight stay.
- Waiting time. Percentage of patients by selected specialities admitted within three months and within 12 months of being listed.
- Operations. Number of patients not admitted within a month of second cancellation of their operation.

The contract should also include details of the clinical processes involved. For example, contracts for chemotherapy could specify that patients should be pain-free to enhance their quality of life.

Types of Contract

In the NHS there are three broad types of contract between purchasers and providers – block, cost and volume, and cost per case. This choice reflects the planning needs of both parties while allowing for a degree of flexibility.

Block

Under this form of contract the HA or GP fundholder pays the service provider an annual fee, in instalments, in return for a defined range of (usually core) services. Such contracts may include some form of indicative workload agreement or fixed volume. For example, for a fixed price, a hospital (the service provider) would agree to undertake all hip replacements required by the Health Authority during the course of the year. In the NHS there are two variants of the block contract – simple and sophisticated. The sophisticated block includes indicative patient activity targets or thresholds with 'floors' and 'ceilings', as well as agreed mechanisms if targets are exceeded. Some elements of case-mix may be included. Such contracts should include quality performance aims and agreements on how the quality, efficiency and outcomes of the services should be monitored.

Block contracts bring benefits to both purchasers and providers. Purchasers benefit from the increased influence that the size of their contracts will bring, as well as competitive pricing which should result in cost efficiency. Providers benefit from the business planning advantages of block contracts, which ensure a steady income and allow for longer-term planning of resources. However, providers may carry out more activity than budgeted for, with no expectation of additional income.

Cost and Volume

Under this type of contract the outputs are specified in terms of patient treatments, rather than in terms of access to services and facilities available. The provider undertakes to provide a clearly defined number of treatments for a fixed 'baseline' price. Beyond that number, funding would be on a cost per case basis, at a level agreed in advance, up to a volume ceiling.

From the providers' point of view, the 'baseline' activity would assist in planning. It also ensures the payment of a reasonable amount for work actually done.

For the purchaser, such contracts also allow for budget planning while leaving a degree of flexibility.

For example, a fundholding practice might expect to require 100 gall bladder excisions during the course of a year. The practice could therefore decide to enter into a contract with the hospital for 80 treatments – allowing for fluctuations in the actual number required and other considerations, such as patients who wish to be treated elsewhere.

Cost and volume contracts therefore allow for greater flexibility and patient choice than block contracts. As with block contracts, quality and outcome measures should be included.

Cost per Case

This type of contract would be used to fund service provision that did not fall into either block or cost and volume contracts. The service provider agrees to provide a range of specified treatments in line with a given contract price for individual patients. Examples would be where a Health Authority or GP fundholder did not have an existing contract with a specific service provider, or where additional treatments were purchased from a contracted provider outside the terms of the existing contract. This would also apply to extra-contractual referrals. Payment would be on a cost per case basis, ideally but not essentially, with prior commitment by either party.

In moving away from simple block contracts the NHS recognizes the need for greater data quality, more accurate costing information and confirmation that interventions are both clinically effective and cost-effective.

Contract Framework

Description of Parties

This section sets out who the contract is between, eg a GP fundholder and a Trust. It may also include who the parties to the contract are, eg the partners in the practice and the chief executive of the hospital Trust.

Objectives

The objectives of the contract should state the services that are to be provided, for example the provision of a defined range of in-patient and day case treatments. In addition, it may be appropriate to specify that the services will be provided to a defined, agreed, level of quality.

It may also be appropriate to insert any nationally or locally agreed targets, eg in England, those from Health of the Nation.

Range of Services

This section should include a general description of the service or services to be provided. This may vary considerably from speciality to speciality and, if necessary, could form a comprehensive list to be added as a schedule to the main contract.

At the end of this section, the parties should have a clear idea of the range and scope of services to be provided, which could include:

- out-patient services at particular locations;
- elective in-patient and facilities for day case surgery;
- the full range of any diagnostic, rehabilitation and non-clinical support services;
- any special investigation techniques;
- health promotion advice;
- arrangements for patients to be referred to other centres if it is in their best interests. There may be separate arrangements made by the purchasers for contracting and payment to other centres (eg a preferred hospice);
- liaison with community healthcare providers and agencies to ensure that the provision of care for the patient on discharge is seamless;
- the development of the integration of primary and secondary care as an important aspect of improving patient care;
- it could be useful for both parties, in developing their roles, to look at ways that agreed clinical guidelines could improve the delivery and effectiveness of care (see Chapter 5).

Quality Specifications

This section may be considered the most important part of the contract. In discussing quality issues, the contracting parties have the opportunity and the flexibility to negotiate to achieve the maximum possible health gain for the patients they represent, improve patients' quality of life and, possibly, reduce purchasers' overall costs in the longer term. This could incorporate preventive and diagnostic treatments of the best quality. There will always be resource constraints, and here priority should be given to services that have measurable outcomes and demonstrable benefits.

Practical steps to take could include:

- Use of medical, clinical and multidisciplinary audit. The purchaser may seek evidence of effectiveness. This may be achieved through audit to address issues leading to improved patient outcome and quality of life, eg the number of post-operative infections and the number of readmissions by speciality.
- Use of clinical or management guidelines. The purchaser may seek evidence of efficiency. This may be achieved by providers working with nationally or locally developed treatment protocols based on best practice or evidence of effectiveness. Use of the results from the Cochrane Centre, National Centre for Reviews and Dissemination of Evidence and the National Centre for Evidence Based Medicine would be appropriate to reassure purchasers that best practice was in place.
- New developments. If any new developments in treatment or clinical management that would significantly affect patient outcome become apparent, purchasers and providers should incorporate these into a revised service, eg an improved local anaesthetic becoming available which would enable a wider range of surgical procedures to be carried out on a day case basis.
- Waiting times. Patients may wish to stipulate maximum guaranteed waiting times for out-patient appointments, admissions and treatments.

Volume and Mix

This section would state the amount of work to be covered by the contract. The development of the contracting process should enable the parties to predict the volume of activity accurately.

The case mix could be based on the severity of the disease, with appropriate allowance for any specific resource allocation where necessary. In addition, the parties should ensure that the services to be purchased are those targeted to the patients' health needs.

Prices

The increasing sophistication of contracts from block to cost and volume has allowed parties to build in greater flexibility and patient choice. For example, a fundholding practice might expect to require 100 gastrectomies during the course of a year. The contract might ultimately provide for 80 treatments to allow for fluctuations in the actual number required as some patients may wish to be treated outside the area. Any additional treatments could be agreed on a cost per case basis. It is important to ensure that all quality and outcome measures are included, regardless of which pricing basis is the most suitable.

Payment Terms

This section sets out the payment arrangements, for example 12 monthly instalments.

Variations to Contract Terms

This sets out what should happen if the contract is not being fulfilled due to circumstances beyond the control of both parties, eg significant changes in the case mix of the anticipated work-load.

Monitoring Arrangements

Agreement should be reached between the parties as to how the contract performance will be monitored and what information should be exchanged to facilitate future contract development and health needs assessment, eg information resulting from audit may be provided to the Director of Public Health.

A key part of the monitoring process is regular meetings between purchasers and providers. Moreover, regular communications may help to prevent any misunderstanding or dispute arising.

Disputes and Arbitration

Contracts in the NHS, where there is no direct management relationship between the parties, are not legally enforceable and, where possible, should be settled by 'in-house' arbitration. This section should therefore specify the procedures to be followed if either party breaches any of the contract terms. For example, suppose the provider fails to submit audit data. It may be agreed that if one party considers that the other has underperformed its obligations, that party will instigate a meeting with the other within two weeks following the meeting, and the non-performing party may be given an agreed time to resolve the issue to the satisfaction of the other party. If the dispute has not been resolved within the agreed period, the other party will have the right of recourse to arbitration.

Contracts with the private sector fall outside the NHS and Community Care Act and so provision must be made for arbitration.

In the event that the dispute cannot be settled it is open to the parties to agree on an external person or body to act as an arbitrator. For example, the regional office of the NHS Executive in which the parties are resident is commonly nominated to act as a conciliator. NB Within the NHS pendulum arbitration is commonly practised by regions, where the findings are in favour of one party or the other, rather than a compromise for both sides.

Content of a Well-written Cost and Volume Contract

1. Well defined in terms of one care group or disease.
2. Comprehensive in terms of providers and services for its care group and disease.

3. Strategic but stable, anticipating planned service changes.
4. Shared with providers, particularly health professionals.
5. Affordable within cash limits.
6. Integrated and patient centred, enabling continuity of care and demonstrating different providers' responsibilities.
7. A means of monitoring and raising service quality, given existing information.
8. Relevant to local circumstances, including GP and patient views.
9. Informed by health needs assessment.
10. Challenging providers to improve service quality and value for money.

The Contracting Process

Several clear steps can be identified in any contracting process. A suitable approach may be to consider the following five.

Step 1. Invitation to Tender

The Health Authority contracts team or GP fundholder will invite hospitals to tender (bid) for a range of services on a block, cost and volume or cost per case basis. The tender document (purchasing intentions and/or purchasing plans) should specify the number of treatments and quality parameters (such as times and clinical processes) required.

When preparing the tender document, which should include as much detail as possible, the Health Authority contracts managers will need to involve GPs in specifying the service required. (Doctors are in the best position to know what their patients want and how these wishes can be met.)

But this first stage of the contract process is not driven solely by the purchaser. Providers must ensure that they are invited to bid for the services in the first place. Hospitals and other providers therefore need to develop marketing approaches that highlight the range and quality of their services.

Step 2. The Offer

Having received and considered the invitation to tender, the provider will then submit a statement of the services it is willing/able to provide, and the price of those services (the service specification). This 'offer' document will have been drawn up following detailed discussions between the hospital contracts staff and the hospital staff providing the services. For clinicians this is the opportunity to state the quality of care they want, and are able, to provide – backed up by clinical audit data.

'Pile it high and sell it cheap' may work in supermarkets, but healthcare services will not be sold on cost alone. Only doctors know the facilities and treatments necessary to achieve the desired standards, and their costs must be built into the contract.

Step 3. Negotiation and Decision

There are likely to be a number of terms in the contract that need clarification or discussion. Further negotiations between the two parties will be required to iron these out. Following these discussions the purchaser will be in a position to consider the final competing bids. The decision on which provider to choose will take into account the providers' ability to meet the quality criteria laid down at an acceptable price.

Step 4. Signing

Once the decision has been made to accept an offer, and each party agrees to all the terms of the contract, then the duly authorized representative of each party will sign the contract document.

Step 5. Monitor Quality and Outcomes

In order to ensure that patients' personal and clinical needs are being met, purchasers will wish to monitor the performance of the provider. There are a number of ways in which this can be done, including the use of patient questionnaires; reports from hospitals on complaints received; and comparison of outcomes with other providers, national averages, best practice, etc.

The increasing use of clinical audit within hospitals will also provide data on the quality outcomes and overall patient care being achieved. Over a period this information will assist in improving shortcomings in the service provided and in negotiating future contracts. The aim should be for a process of continuous improvement.

Involvement

The key to the whole contracts process is the involvement at every stage of all those purchasing or providing the service.

Fundholding GPs already contract for a proportion of hospital and community based services. It is essential that non-fundholding GPs also play a role in specifying the services they require for their patients. Equally, hospital clinicians need to be fully involved in the contracting process, to ensure the service specifications are achievable and detail best practice.

Only by involving those directly responsible for referring patients and providing the service will contracts fully address the needs of the patient.

Tips

1. Get out and meet the people with whom you are contracting.
2. Involve both managers and clinicians in the negotiating meetings.
3. Use negotiation – not confrontation (look for a 'win-win' solution).
4. Build in quality standards – in contracts, measures and outcomes could include the use of anti-emetics for patients undergoing chemotherapy, as a specific clinical quality measure, as well as broader measures describing waiting times, meals, etc.

'Purchasing for health gain is undoubtedly the most difficult but also the most intellectually challenging job of the reformed NHS.' (Dr Diana Walford, NHSE)

Overcoming Barriers

Effective Contracting

The contract between purchasers and providers must be effective to ensure best use of available NHS resources in terms of money, manpower and time. Those who are evaluating the effectiveness of the NHS reforms have identified the main barriers to effective contracting as being:

1. Inadequate patient information.
2. Lack of case-mix measures.
3. Absence of reasonably accurate and practical costing systems.
4. Few common and measurable quality factors.

The importance of improving healthcare contracting has been recognized and the matter is being given much higher priority both nationally and locally, with suggestions being made to improve the content of contracts and the contracting process.

Inadequate Patient Information

A number of recent innovations will improve the quality of patient information available. These include:

1. The planned introduction of a unique patient identifier in 1996.
2. Total fundholding/total purchasing pilots, enabling computer capture of much data and information on patients in primary care.
3. Improved hospital information systems, covering the whole range of services.
4. Developments in community information systems, covering the care of patients in their own homes.

These should assist in developing the quality of morbidity information held on patient populations, in addition to existing mortality data. Consequently, information on epidemiology, clinical health need and Health Service usage can be matched to enable planning and contracting to be more accurate. In turn this will improve the quality of information available on health status, both of individual patients and of populations.

Lack of Case-mix Measures

One of the problems for purchasers and providers is in planning for the variety of severity and complexity in patients presenting for treatment of a particular condition. For example, the most common workload measure in acute care contracting is the 'finished consultant episode'. This does not differentiate between relatively minor cases with lengths of stay of, say, two days, and those cases that require much more expensive treatment and care for periods of two or three weeks. This is being addressed by the introduction and use of healthcare resource groups (HRGs). These group patients into just over 500 categories, which are designed to give a picture of patient related activity, which can be equated with resource consumption. These are currently available for acute services and work has started on developing case-mix groupings for out-patient, ambulatory and community care.

Presenting provider clinicians with their workload for a resident population in case-mix format enables discussions to be held on treating case-mix more effectively by:

- reducing lengths of stay;
- transferring work from in-patient to day cases;
- ensuring that the case mix was banded to the correct price bands (see costing systems);
- supporting people in the community, rather than admitting them to hospital;
- preventing inappropriate admissions.

Absence of Accurate and Practical Costing Systems

The GP fundholding scheme requires hospitals to publish their prices for the list of elective surgical procedures included in the scheme. These prices, and the lengths of stay on which they are based, have highlighted wide and expensive variations in clinical practice which do not appear to be justified on the basis of outcomes.

There are a number of areas in which changes to costing practices are being explored. Costed HRGs are a finance driven way of classifying and costing provider activities. Interventions recorded using OPCS (Office of Population, Census and Surveys) and ICD (International Classification of Diseases) codes are grouped together if they are clinically similar. In the acute sector some work has been undertaken to provide costings for HRGs in the orthopaedics, gynaecology and ophthalmology specialities.

This work is extending to other acute specialities and throughout the NHS and should be completed for the contracting round 1997/98. This information, once it is available below speciality, will enable providers to compare how well they are performing in comparison with others, identify areas for improvement and identify areas of high efficiency. Developments by the National Case Mix Office (NCMO) have the objective of making proposals for HRGs in the areas of need, resource use and prognosis for both the acute and non-acute sector.

Resource allocation and projections provide information on the funds available for hospital, community and primary care services. Allocations are made, currently to Health Authorities and GP fundholders through HCHS (Hospital and Community Health Sevices), FHS (Family Health Services) and GPFH allocations. Planning future resources depends on changes in the size and scope of fundholding scheme, HCHS and FHS and the effects locally of changes for funding of education, training, research, long-stay elderly patients, etc.

In addition, other factors affecting future resource investment will include community area changes, medical technology, and change in clinical practice, Health of the Nation targets, etc.

Price banding systems to reflect case-mix are useful in reflecting the wide variations of work within specialities, ensuring price really equals cost and to avoid planned cross-subsidization. This has been successfully used in Wandsworth since 1991.

Invitations to tender apply to contracts for services valued at over £100,000, lower in some areas. NHS providers are required to complete their information by including details on alternative suppliers for the service.

Market testing aims to secure better value for money in the provision of public services. Private–public joint ventures are to be encouraged. There is no longer any requirement to assess proposed joint ventures against a hypothetical, fully NHS-funded alternative. Market testing for the private provision of services need only make comparisons with public sector provision if the latter is a realistic possibility within the proposed timescales.

Minimum standards for costing by providers deal with:

- the classification of all costs into fixed, semi-fixed and variable categories;
- the analysis of all costs, either as directly allocable to a speciality or as indirect costs or overheads to be subsequently apportioned;
- the methods of apportionment/allocation of all costs to individual specialities.

The implementation of costing and contracting, outlined in FDL (Finance Directive Letter (94) 53), is only one of a number of changes affecting contract prices, which are all occurring simultaneously. Other changes include:

- evolution to more sophisticated types of contract (towards cost and volume – described on page 128);
- adjustments to contracted activity levels (including recognition of what has already happened or resulting from improved recording of activity);
- efficiency gains/cash releasing savings;
- correction of previous contract errors.

Few Common and Measurable Quality Factors

The focus on quality in the NHS needs to move from detailed specification of service standards around process issues to a more patient centred approach.

The pursuit of quality measures in the NHS covers a range of areas:

- measurable outcomes, incorporating clinical effectiveness;
- Patients' Charter criteria;
- Health of the Nation;
- chronic disease management;
- core common standards;

- sanctions and incentives;
- clinical audit;
- guidelines (eg best practice for treatment and referral).

Executive Letter guidance on contracting (EL (94) 88) states that purchasers and providers 'must ensure that doctors, nurses and other professionals from provider units are actively involved in the contracting process.' The value of their involvement is in developing clearer service specifications/protocols, influencing the development of quality targets and influencing the pattern of activity. They are also key to the effective management and monitoring of contract performance.

As part of the drive towards use of best practice interventions, purchasers were required for 1995/96 to reduce investment in two areas shown to be clinically ineffective. In this way purchasing will drive the service towards those interventions that deliver measurable health gain.

To date, only around 20 per cent of acute contracts demonstrate a disease-focused element, usually in Health of the Nation areas. Progress in this area is likely to be made over the next few years, particularly as the quality of data on morbidity improves.

Incentives and sanctions are currently largely financial and have been used around data quality, timeliness of confirmation, waiting times, activity levels, quality standards and, occasionally, around discharge arrangements. 'Quality and Contracting – taking the agenda forward' (NHS, 1994) suggests that there could be beneficial effects if purchasers concentrated on incentives or the absence of incentives rather than sanctions. A bonus payment is just one approach, but rewards may also include support for a capital project, longer-term contracts or equipment.

Effective monitoring arrangements may include the specification of a limited number of core standards. In some parts of the country, eg Trent Region, purchasers have agreed to include between 20 and 30 core common quality standards with providers. Existing mechanisms for monitoring include organizational and clinical audit and accreditation (eg BS 5750/ISO 9000).

Contracting for Community Care

Community care requires a much more sophisticated contracting approach than that provided by block contracts. Community contracts must be sensitive to individual need and individually costed packages of care. Contract budgets may need to be devolved to locality purchasers, matching those of social care managers. GPs as purchasers clearly have a role to play in this context, creating the tactical commissioning capacity to match the strategic contribution of Health Authorities.

These requirements indicate that not only is a mature working relationship important between purchasers and providers, but that all groups of purchasers must work closely together – Social Services, GPFHs, HAs and other agencies who commission a range of services covering acute, mental health, learning disabilities, community health, ambulance and counselling services.

Croydon Community Trust is piloting 'contracting for intermediate outcomes', which has the added advantage of involving users in decisions about their care, eg in people with leg ulcers the intermediate outcome may be the average rate at which patients' ulcers heal. Providers can then bid for money to improve leg ulcer healing rates by an agreed percentage.

Purchaser/Provider Contract Template

This is a suggested format for a contract between a purchaser and a provider for the provision of asthma care. It includes standards for clinical and management outcomes that are now regarded as a high priority within the NHS.

Scope

The agreement covers the following services:

- all in-patient, day case, and out-patient workload, previously purchased by the HA;
- all diagnostic and therapeutic services associated with the above;
- accident and emergency services.

The Trust agrees to provide all the resources required for the provision of the services outlined above and agrees not to subcontract any part of these services without consultation and agreement of the purchaser.

Contract Type

This is a cost per case contract, with monthly payments based on activity that both parties agree has taken place; or this is a cost and volume contract, with an agreed activity and caseload mix for the year.

Invoicing

For a cost per case contract, the following invoice agreement is standard.

The provider undertakes to send out-patient minimum data set information on the 10th of each month following that to which the activity applies. The provider will undertake to make available in-patient minimum data sets, accompanied by invoices on the 20th of each month following that to which the activity applies.

Purchasers will reconcile the value of the work that has taken place on their behalf, minus the value of 'queried work' to the invoice value, correcting the invoice if necessary. Invoices must be returned to the unit by the last day of the month following the month to which they apply.

Formal invoices will be authorised for HA/HB/GPFH payment within X weeks of receipt.

The provider agrees to waive all charges for episodes not invoiced within X weeks of the end of the month in which the episode is completed unless by prior arrangement.

For a cost and volume contract the purchaser will pay one-twelfth of the agreed annual amount every month.

Notification of Treatment/Attendance

a) **Out-patients**   Each out-patient attendance will be followed by a communication containing the following information:

- patient name and identifier;
- date of episode;

- speciality;
- confirmation of discharge from out-patients department or further follow-up;
- confirmation of waiting list if appropriate and whether listing is as out-patient, day case or in-patient;
- consultants will send a clinical letter after every out-patient attendance.

(b) In-patient/day case   Each completed in-patient episode will be followed within X weeks by a written clinical letter containing the following information:

- patient name and identifier;
- date of admission;
- procedure details and whether day care or in-patient;
- mode of admission, eg emergency or routine;
- whether listed for further treatment.

Waiting Lists and Monitoring

The purchaser will choose which of their non-urgent patients on the waiting list they wish to be treated, and the following protocol describes the responsibilities of purchaser and provider in achieving this: [A detailed description of the provider's system is then described.]

Quality

The following principles will apply:

Equity   Treatment should be offered on the patient's capacity to benefit only, ie provided to address greatest need, assessed clinically and socially.

Efficiency   Providers will be expected to meet year-on-year cost improvement and efficiency targets.

Access   Specification of service locations defines the purchaser's expectations of geographical access; Patients' Charter standards will apply to waiting times.

Effectiveness and appropriateness These are measured through the use of audit and appropriate outcome measures.

Social acceptability This contract is informed by the purchaser's strategy for health which has been subject to local consultation. Patient satisfaction with services can be used as a further indicator of social acceptability.

All services should be delivered within a framework of technical, professional and managerial competence.

Additionally, the purchaser is assured that:

- Processes are in place to develop continuous improvements in standards. The programme is available to purchasers.
- Clinical audit is in place and is informing the process of patient care. Aggregated results of audit activity will routinely be provided to purchasers.
- Policies and procedures have been developed and are being implemented in the following areas:
  - communication with patients and between disciplines, including general practice;
  - admission and discharge of patients.

The purchaser will have sight of each of these policy and procedure documents together with the results of annual audit of their implementation.

Disease-specific Quality Measures – Asthma

Prevalence: About 1.7 million people in the UK suffer from asthma.

Mortality: 2,000 adult deaths a year in England and Wales; 38% of fatalities were under 65 years of age; an estimated 40,000 years of potential life lost; asthma is the only 'avoidable' cause of death that has an increasing mortality rate.

Morbidity: 50% of asthmatics aged 5 to 65 years report breathlessness at least once a week; 39% are woken every night by their asthma; 50% of adult asthmatics suffer an acute attack at least once a year; 100,000 asthmatics are hospitalized each year, 92% of them due to emergency admission.

Cost: £400 million to the NHS in total, 20% of which was incurred by secondary care; £60 million in sickness benefit; £350 million in lost productivity.

Asthma in primary care

The vast majority of asthma patients can be managed effectively within the primary care/community care setting. This requires good management, treatment and education. Secondary care will therefore only be required for a small number of patients with unstable, problematic, severe asthma or acute life-threatening episodes.

Diagnosis: A diagnosis can normally be made on the basis of clinical history, physical examination and a demonstration of reversible airways obstruction.

Treatment: National guidelines have been produced by the BTS (British Thoracic Society) which can be adapted for local use. This has been done for the purposes of this contract (see pages 68–70 for asthma management guidelines).

Referral criteria – non-acute cases

Adults: poor control, despite adequate therapy; requirement for long-term oral steroids; requirement for long-term nebulised bronchodilators; sudden life-threatening asthma; diagnostic doubt.

Paediatrics: diagnostic doubt; poor control, despite good inhaler technique and compliance; parental request for a second opinion; brittle asthma; requirement for long-term high dose steroids; more than four courses of oral steroids in one year; an infant with severe or persistent symptoms.

Referral criteria – acute admissions

Adults: Any life-threatening features; exhaustion, silent chest, bradycardia, cyanosis. Less than or equal to 33% predicted PEFR (peak expiratory flow rate). A poor response after 15–30 minutes to nebulised beta agonist and oxygen. More than one of the following: afternoon/evening attack, recent hospitalization, previous severe attacks, patient unable to assess symptoms, difficult social conditions.

Paediatric: Any life-threatening features; fatigue, exhaustion, agitation or reduced consciousness, cyanosis, silent chest or poor respiratory effort. PEFR 33% or less of predicted or best. Poor response to nebulised beta agonist after 10 minutes (PEFR still less than 50%). Inability of the child to take treatment. Severe breathlessness or tiredness. More than one of the following symptoms: evening consultation, recent nocturnal symptoms, previous severe attacks, family unable to assess symptom severity.

Asthma services provided by Trust

- Out-patient care, including shared care programme.
- In-patient care.
- Accident and emergency.

Objectives and outcomes
In line with the national goals of asthma management, our objectives and outcomes will be to:

- recognize and diagnose asthma accurately;
- abolish the symptoms of asthma;
- restore best possible or normal lung function;
- reduce the risks of further attacks;
- adhere to agreed treatment guidelines unless clinically otherwise indicated;
- deliver services that are judged by X per cent of purchasers and patients who receive them to be satisfactory or better;
- deliver services within the standards identified within the Patients' Charter.

Measures of achievement

- Measurable improvements in symptoms, measured by routine symptom scoring.
- Measurable improvements in lung function.
- Reduced numbers of readmissions for severe attacks.
- X per cent of patients following agreed treatment guidelines.
- Positive purchaser responses to the above results.
- High satisfaction ratings from questionnaires.
- Achievement of Patients' Charter waiting times targets.

Non-compliance

A number of factors may arise during the year that could affect the ability of either party to fulfil its obligations under the contract.

Demand for specified services outstrips contracted levels beyond agreed treatment levels.
Action: Where there is evidence of significant in-year changes in demand, activity levels will be renegotiated on the understanding that additional activity will be purchased at marginal cost.

Demand for emergency services impedes the provider's ability to deliver elective services.
Action: Emergency services should be protected. The purchaser should be informed within X working days and corrective action agreed.

Unforeseen cost pressures.
Action: The provider would normally be expected to absorb cost pressures in year. In exceptional cases the matter should be placed on the agenda of the next scheduled monitoring meeting.

Unforeseeable issues.
Action: Unforeseeable issues that threaten the ability of either party to comply with the contract terms should be discussed at scheduled monitoring meetings. In exceptional circumstances, where the matter is urgent and threatens the contract's overall objectives, an extraordinary meeting of the contracting parties should be arranged.

In the event that agreement cannot be reached on remedial action to address non-compliance with agreed terms, arbitration will be attempted through the usual channels.

Where the purchaser is forced to make alternative contracting arrangements to protect overall objectives, appropriate adjustments will be made to the contract price.

Monitoring

Meetings between the contracted parties will be held at intervals of X months to consider progress. Information will be supplied

on: objectives and outcomes; audit results from symptom monitoring; data on lung function tests; numbers of admissions and
readmissions due to asthma; exception reporting on patients
treated outside guidelines; six-monthly report on out-patients'
waiting times; responses to satisfaction questionnaires; quality;
quality programme for continuous improvement; policy and
procedure documents; exception reports to policy and procedure
implementation; aggregated results of clinical audit; high
level performance indicators; outputs; summary of services delivered (monthly); condition-specific contract minimum data sets
(quarterly).

Table 8.1 Planning year

	Purchasers	**Providers**
September	Publish initial purchasing plans and contracting intentions.	Inform purchasers of major changes to pricing structure. Submit draft strategic directions.
October		Submit business cases for capital investment.
November	Submit draft/outline corporate contract to Region.	Publish initial/first cut prices. Submit draft business plans.
January	Agree finalized contracting intentions with providers.	Provide finalized prices to purchasers.
March	**Agree all contracts between purchasers and providers**	
	Make purchasing plans public.	Publish strategic direction.

Quality Initiatives

Apart from the quality dimension of the contracting process there
are a number of mechanisms that can be used to attract and
enhance quality in the NHS. Quality is a huge subject, but this
section concentrates on three areas: quality as a goal in the NHS;
the monitoring and measurement of quality in contracts; quality
as a topic for training and education.

Quality as a Goal in the NHS

The first question is, 'What does quality mean to the NHS?' To some it could be one of the biggest and most impenetrable questions for the service. There are any number of 'quality gurus' preaching their brand of quality initiative to a receptive NHS audience, and it would be easy to get bogged down in the terminology. It is very tempting to recite TQM or CQI as a mantra at the start of any busy executive's day!

Behind all the quality consultants' rhetoric there are some sound principles, which are reflected in much of what the NHS says it desires to achieve; for example, in the values expressed by one region, derived from work by the King's Fund:

- Equitable – equal treatment for equal need.
- Accessible – ready access to services needed.
- Effective – achievement of intended benefit.
- Appropriate – relevant to need.
- Efficient – resources used to best effect.
- Responsive – reflect reasonable expectations.

Quality here is reflected in the desire to achieve both quality in the care provided to patients and quality of life and health improvements to patients themselves.

Providers who can demonstrate a commitment to quality will be well placed to survive in the new-look NHS. Devices for this can include accreditation, eg King's Fund Organizational Audit, Chartermark, BS 5750, ISO 9000 – all indicators of a pursuit of quality.

The quality agenda in the NHS is characterized by:

1. A desire to improve standards of care towards best practice. This is reflected in the content of Els, purchasing plans and service specifications from around the country. Academic centres support this work, eg HSMU Manchester with the Longman publication *Best Practice in Healthcare Commissioning* (Sheaff and Peel, 1993).
2. A move away from activity measures to outcome and effectiveness measures (although the planned publication of the amended efficiency index to include measures of effectiveness has been delayed to the Autumn of 1996).

3. Activities by the Royal Colleges and 'professional groupings', addressing clinical variation and evidence-based decision making. The information on clinical variation is being put to practical use by, eg Greater Glasgow Health Board in deciding where to award contracts.

4. Patients' Charter and increasing consumer involvement in healthcare choices. Interestingly, the role of CHCs is under current focus, with changes implemented in April 1996. There is still an issue over what the NHS can practically consult on. Research to date indicates a number of consultation exercises that were based on confirming decisions already taken by the Authority, rather than in areas where choices can be made based on public input.

5. A desire for improved communication between primary and secondary care – a true seamless service, incorporating referral and discharge. We have already seen parts of the country where guidelines are being developed which are patient centred rather than service centred. This can help in eliminating duplicated diagnostic tests and other areas of potential waste.

6. Calls for decision making based on effectiveness, efficiency and appropriateness. The arrival of the Effectiveness Bulletins and the growing number of new journals on effectiveness are a way of pulling together information that has, up to now, been dealt with on a piecemeal basis, and not widely adopted in current practice.

7. A wish for clarification of roles and accountabilities, both for management and the medical and allied professions. For example, the change in the role of managers employed by the Health Authorities requires a change from a purchasing perspective to a strategy and monitoring perspective.

So the ground is set for quality to be addressed in a systematic way. One of the most appropriate vehicles for getting quality into the system is through the purchaser/provider contractual arrangement, which was covered earlier.

The NHS is taking some steps to provide quality integrated into its activities. In non-clinical areas, for example, partnerships exist with building and facilities management, construction, provision of laundry and catering services. A question here is 'Do these arrangements mirror the in-depth partnership approach adopted by the Lane Group and Body Shop?' (described as being one of the most advanced forms of partnership in the commercial world).

Of course it is easy for a commercial organization to talk about outcomes. In manufacturing they equal zero defects; in service provision – timeliness and appropriateness, as demonstrated in the Body Shop example.

Ultimately, sales and profit can be identified as the outcomes required, but built into that is a recognition of quality. If quality is poor sales will not result, industry will not generate repeat business and its reputation will suffer. And industry has to be clear about *what* it is selling to its market place – quality products or services.

Monitoring and Measurement of Quality in Contracts

Having considered what the NHS means by quality, the next area to cover is how it is measured and monitored, both in the content of the contracts themselves and, more importantly, when the providers implement the requirements of the contract.

There are a number of ways of monitoring both the quality of care given to patients and their change in health status, bearing in mind that there is not always a causal relationship between the two. Many of these techniques can be employed to determine the effectiveness of the contract. They can be ranked in increasing order of objectivity and rigorousness, starting with a useful, but very subjective, method.

1. Anecdotal evidence can be valuable to confirm or refute other information sources. However, by itself it is not a robust tool, because one anecdote could easily be countered by another demonstrating a different viewpoint. Collecting a range of anecdotes and weighing the information is useful.
2. Complaints and compliments: as general practice is also required to have a procedure in place from April 1996 this could prove an increasingly useful source of information on the quality of services given. However, it is as well to remember that our culture is one where we are reluctant to complain at all, so the number of complaints may be quite small in

comparison to the number of procedures or treatments provided. We are even more reticent to give praise, so compliments are also likely to be thin on the ground.

3. Case studies involve a staff member shadowing the patient through their stay and recording their impressions as they go through the experience. A well-documented example of this can be found in John Ovretveit's *Health Service Quality*, published in 1992, but containing much of value today.

4. In-depth patient interviews: where patients have received more complex treatment, perhaps involving more than one specialty.

5. Patient surveys are appropriate for where a large number of patients have received a relatively simple or straightforward procedure, and where a quantitative result can be generated. This will be in addition to the subjective assessment information, which is qualitative, from the patients' own perspective.

6. Audits, ie measuring the outputs in terms of improved (or otherwise) patient outcomes.

7. Research: for example, where the value of a new or experimental procedure is being assessed. This is the most objective and rigorous of the types of assessment, but is still subject to observer bias and application of individual judgement.

Taken as a whole, these various methods can be used to monitor and evaluate the effectiveness, efficiency and appropriateness of different services for patients. No one method should be relied on exclusively; each will add a different dimension to the monitoring process.

Once the quality of a service has been characterized, there are a number of ways to make that explicit. One is regulation, usually by a government associated organization, which will lay down minimum standards and then monitor provider activities against them. This is a route chosen by other healthcare systems around the world. There are a number of drawbacks to this form of quality monitoring, in that once an organization has demonstrated compliance to such fixed standards withdrawal of registered status would lead to severe financial consequences for the provider concerned. In addition the standards themselves, while able to be improved over time, are relatively fixed and therefore slow to respond to changes in care delivery that will improve quality.

As I said earlier, another of the proposed mechanisms is accreditation of providers, and a number of possible options are available here. In countries such as Canada national accreditation bodies are moving from minimum to optimal achievable standards, which are defined as 'the best possible level that can be achieved given the available resources'. In the UK there is not the same national mechanism in place, but a plethora of measures, both Health Service specific and more general accreditation.

Both primary care and secondary care providers have sought and obtained BS 5750 accreditation and the international equivalent, ISO 9000 and its developments. This is a general quality measure that applies to service-related organizations. It, together with the King's Fund Organizational Audit, looks at the structure and processes associated with service delivery, with little monitoring of the outputs or outcomes of care. The criteria of the more Health Service-specific initiatives are likely to change with the increasing evidence to support best practice in healthcare. The other observation to make about the current systems in place in the UK is that they have been created and monitored with little clinical input, which brings us to the last of the three areas looking at quality in the NHS.

Quality as an Education and Training Topic

This is not, of course, strictly part of the contracting process, but providers demonstrating a commitment to education and training will be well placed to support improved clinical and management practices. It therefore fits well, both for managers and clinicians.

All clinicians undertake postgraduate education, and GPs currently receive an allowance for this. The system for postgraduate training in both primary and secondary care is currently being reviewed. The quality of clinical care and maintaining current best practice knowledge will ensure that improvements in services for patients and their resulting state of health should increase. As a starting point, work in both medical and clinical audit has already shown changes in clinical practice resulting from the use of a systematic process of review of current practice. There is some discussion as to how this education and training activity can be used to ensure that patients will receive the best available care within the resources available. Such discussion has recently focused on the idea of reaccreditation of clinicians, which takes the concept of post-graduate training further.

So what does all this mean for you? I would suggest that this is one of the key priorities for both commissioning and providing organizations, whether at general practice level or serving a population approaching one million people. You could usefully ask yourself:

- Do I have meaningful quality measures in my contracts?
- Are they being monitored with the same vigour that is applied to the financial aspects of the arrangement?
- Am I committed to using education and training as a means of improving quality in the services I purchase or provide?

With the proposed addition of reaccreditation requirements for clinicians there will be some organizational consequences in terms of what information should be made available to purchasers to assist their purchasing decisions.

Chapter 9

Role of the Board

Boards are part of the infrastructure for both purchaser and provider organizations in the NHS.

Often their role is indistinct and it is only recently, through the work of the NAHAT Centre for Board Development, that the role of the Board in the planning process has become clearer.

> 'What's the difference between a supermarket trolley and a non-executive director? One has a mind of its own and the other you fill with food and drink.' (*Bulletpoint*, 1995)

This somewhat frivolous observation may indeed be how NHS organizations view the Board and its members. However, Boards have a key role to play both in the creation of the business plan and in its implementation. In the first place, the production of the plan is the responsibility of the Authority as a whole. By involving all staff, there will be an increased commitment to ensuring the plan is achieved. This involvement includes the chair and non-executives as much as the executive members of the Authority or Trust.

Functions of the Board

NHS Boards have six key functions for which they are held accountable by the NHS Executive on behalf of the Secretary of State. They were recommended by the corporate governance steering group and accepted by the Secretary of State:

1. To set the strategic direction of the organization within the overall policies and priorities of the government and the NHS, define its annual and longer-term objectives and agree plans to achieve them. (This confirms the active part Board members should play in the organization's planning activity.)
2. To oversee the delivery of planned results by monitoring performance against objectives and ensuring corrective action is taken when necessary. (This indicates the responsibility of the Board in monitoring the implementation of the plan.)
3. To ensure effective financial stewardship through value for money, financial control and financial planning and strategy. (These are tests to be applied to the objectives and action plans, ensuring that NHS resources are used wisely.)
4. To ensure that high standards of corporate governance and personal behaviour are maintained in the conduct of the business as a whole organization. (This encapsulates aspects of the mission statement and answers the question 'Why would we be proud to work for this organization?' It also sets the agenda for ensuring that the organization complies with rules (on openness, corporate governance, probity, etc) and adheres to the less formal rules with which the internal market operates.)
5. To appoint, appraise and remunerate senior executives. (The Board's role here is to ensure that the organization's management is capable of developing robust plans. This area is potentially full of tension, between non-executives and executives of the organization, and requires diplomacy and tact to resolve.)
6. To ensure that there is effective dialogue between the organization and the local community in its plans and performance and that these are responsive to the community's needs. (This confirms the significance of the rise in consumerism as a key environmental trend for the NHS.)

In summary, the Board's role should be seen as helping to set and monitor the performance of the organization against its mission, values and objectives – a knowledge based function, rather than a policing one.

There are a number of key issues associated with Boards. These include the level of involvement they wish to have, or are able to have in working with the Authority or Trust and the level of communication they wish to have with the organization. It is necessary for Board members to view themselves as a team, which will help in carrying out their role of stewardship. They will also fulfil the role of an objective eye when difficult decisions are needed, for example in ensuring that obligations for efficiency gains are met. They have a role in assessing the effectiveness of the organization and in determining an appropriate size for it – important in considering joint working, alliances and possible mergers (as with the integration of FHSA and DHA in England during 1995 and 1996).

To tackle this sizeable agenda, Boards have taken a number of approaches. They have tried not to devolve everything to the executives, or individually or collectively to do the job of the executives. In some areas Board members adopt an area of interest in a mentoring role for aspects of the Authority's business. Suggested areas for mentoring include audit committee, complaints procedure, consumer surveys, legal matters, financial matters (including the budget), equal opportunity, Health of the Nation, Patients' Charter, Children's Act, residential homes and primary care led NHS strategy. The Board member (chosen either because of professional background or personal interest) works with the senior management member responsible for the relevant policy.

Another Board activity has been to ensure the integration of the business plan, Trust plan and the corporate contract, in which the 'givens' from the centre are addressed and incorporated. In addition, because of the basis on which Boards are appointed, they need to ensure they maintain their independence without appearing austere and distant from the organization for which they have stewardship.

Involvement of the Board in the Planning Process

I have worked with a number of NHS organizations over the last few years, both purchasers and providers. This work has involved Board members in addition to executives, and it is clear that they are interested in the 'What' question – what is it that the organization is and what does it do? Board members are less interested in the 'How' question, when it comes to the level of detail needed to assign objectives and responsibilities for the organization. So, looking back to the original planning chart, the parts of the process that Board members can most usefully get involved in are the generation of the mission for the organization, its values, the SWOT analysis, key issues and critical success factors. They can make significant contributions to the direction of the organization both from a professional and personal perspective.

The Board's Role in Plan Implementation

Board members are usually well connected in the local community and can do much to assist in communicating the plan and its consequences to the local population. So they, individually and collectively, can do much to manage stakeholders. Additionally, their role in the implementation phase of the planning process revolves around monitoring the performance of the organization against the plan. Regular reviews are an effective way of spotting deviations from the original plan and identifying signals where one of the contingencies may need to be put into effect.

The Board is one of the greatest assets NHS organizations have, whether purchasers or providers. They are a resource that can be used effectively to ensure the survival and success of your organization.

Glossary

Collaborative working Collaborative working is a process that involves two parties (supplier and customer, or two organizations) working together to identify needs and discuss possible solutions. Each party can then assess the risks and benefits of proceeding with the projects and map out the most appropriate way forward. The key concepts involved are: the concept of win–win; jointly agreed shared objectives; shared risk and benefit; and honesty and openness on both sides, ie the ability to walk away from the project.

Commissioning The strategic activity of assessing needs, resources and current services, and developing a strategy to make best use of available resources.

Disease management Disease management is the acquisition and delivery of all healthcare interventions relevant to the prevention and treatment of a disease, in order to optimize both health and economic outcomes.

Evidence-based medicine This is an aspect of medical practice that compiles the 'best available' evidence on the effectiveness (clinical and management) of interventions; the results are then disseminated for practitioners to adopt as 'best practice' or, even better, 'usual practice'.

Joint commissioning The process in which two or more commissioning agencies act together to coordinate their commissioning, taking joint responsibility for translating strategy into action. This will generally involve health, Social Services, housing, education and other agencies.

Joint provision Differs from joint commissioning, but can be the result of joint commissioning or purchasing, where agencies jointly provide a service. Joint provision is not the only, nor necessarily the most appropriate, outcome from joint commissioning.

Joint purchasing Often used when discussing joint commissioning, it describes the situation where two or more agencies coordinate the actual buy-in of services, preferably in the context of joint commissioning and a shared strategy.

Managed care Managed care is an approach to healthcare delivery that links the financing of care and the delivery of care to benefit patients.

Purchasing The operational activity, set within the context of commissioning, of applying resources to buy services in order to meet needs – either at a macro/population level or at a micro/individual level.

Bibliography and Further Reading

NHS

Bower, P (1995) personal communication.

Deffenbaugh, J (1990) 'Debunking the plans bunkum', *Health Service Journal*.

Department of Health (1990) *Health Service Developments: Working for Patients; Medical Audit in the Famliy Practitioners*, Circular HC(FP)(90)8, DoH, London.

Drummond, MF and Maynard, A (eds) (1993) *Purchasing and Providing Cost-effective Health Care*, Churchill Livingstone, London.

Dukes, JA and Stewart, R (1994) *The Use and Usefulness of Guidelines*, Oxford Healthcare Management Institute, Oxford.

Eddy, D (1992) 'Cost-effectiveness Analysis: A Conversation with my Father', *JAMA*, March, 267, 12: 1669–75.

Ellis J, Mulligan, I, Rowe, J and Sackett, D (1995) 'Inpatient General Medicine is Evidence Based', *Lancet*, 346: 407–10.

Fry, J (1993) *General Practice – The Facts*, Radcliffe Medical Press, Oxford.

Grol, R (1993) 'Development of Clinical Guidelines for General Practice Care', *British Journal of General Practice*, 43: 146–51.

Ham, C (1991) *The New National Health Service – Organization and Management*, Radcliffe Medical Press, Oxford.

Ham, C (1994) *Management and Competition in the New NHS*, Radcliffe Medical Press, Oxford.

Hatcher, P (1995) 'Managed Care in the UK Health Services', *Management Centre Newsletter*, October, 1, 3: 1–2.

Lakhani, A (1994) *Population Health Outcomes Model*, DoH, London.

NHS Executive Purchasing Unit (1994) *Quality and Contracting, Taking the Agenda Forward*, NHS Executive, Leeds.

Ovretveit, J (1992) *Health Service Quality*, Blackwell Scientific Publications, Oxford.

Roe, P and Semple Piggot, C (1994) *Health Gain and How to Achieve It*, Glaxo Pharmaceuticals, London.

Scottish Office (1995) *Clinical and Cost-effectiveness: Consultation Paper on Roles and Relationships*, February.

Sheaff, WR and Peel, VJ (1993) *Best Practice in Healthcare Commissioning*, Longman, London.

Warner, M, Riley, C, Pullen, A and Semple Piggot, C (eds) (1995) *Releasing Resources to Achieve Health Gain*, Radcliffe Medical Press, Oxford.

Wilkin, D, Hallam, K and Doggett, MA (1992) *Measures of Need and Outcome for Primary Health Care*, Oxford University Press, Oxford.

Business and Management

Hamel, G and Prahalad, CK (1989) in *Harvard Business Review*, May/June: 63.

Hunningher, E (ed.) (1986) *The Manager's Handbook*, Marshall Editions, London.

Johnson, G and Scholes, K (1993) *Exploring Corporate Strategy*, Prentice-Hall, London.

Majaro, S (1988) *The Creative Gap – Managing Ideas for Profit*, Longman, Harlow.

Normann, R and Ramirez, R (1993) in *Harvard Business Review*, July/August: 65.

Obeng, E (1994) *All Change – The Project Leader's Secret Handbook*, Pitman Publishing, London.

Shaw, W and Day, G (1987) *The Businessman's Complete Checklist*, Hutchinson Business, London.

General

Carroll, L (1991) *Alice's Adventures in Wonderland*, Oxford University Press, Oxford.

Index